mid life

Redefined

To my mum, for inspiring me.

To my girls, Daisy, Poppy and Ruby Rose, for motivating me.

And to all the amazing women redefining midlife. Yes, that's you.

And to Emily.

About the author

Alana Kirk is a life and leadership coach, writer and journalist. As the Midlife Coach, she encourages and empowers women to take advantage of this extraordinary midlife. She is the author of the bestselling memoir *The Sandwich Years: A Story of Love, Loss and Dirty Dishes*, has written for Irish and UK publications and taken part in radio and TV panels. Alana lives in Dublin with her three daughters.

mid life *Redefined*

Better, Bolder, Brighter.

ALANA KIRK

Dancing Publishing

First published in 2022 by
Dancer Publishing
Dublin
Ireland
themidlifecoach.org

Amazon paperback edition ISBN: 978 1 78846 242 6
Paperback ISBN: 978 1 78846 240 2
eBook ISBN: 978 1 78846 241 9

A CIP catalogue record for this book is
available from the British Library

Produced by Kazoo Independent Publishing Services
222 Beech Park, Lucan, Co. Dublin
kazoopublishing.com

Kazoo Independent Publishing Services is not the publisher of this work. All rights and responsibilities pertaining to this work remain with Dancer Publishing.

Cover design by Andrew Brown

Printed in the EU

CONTENTS

SECTION THREE – ACTION

INTRODUCTION

★

NEVER MIND THE ANSWER, *Am I Asking* THE RIGHT QUESTION?

I don't mean the question that quivers on the lips of most of us women at midlife: where the hell am I, and how did I get here? (Followed quickly by challenging conundrums such as: Can I wear boyfriend jeans if I don't have a boyfriend?, and why is it that every time I ransack my underwear drawer I can't find knickers that are sexy *and* comfortable?). The question might be one you are already starting to ask yourself, if not with these actual words, but in some vague form. That question is the reason you've picked up this book. Or maybe, you aren't asking it yet but you know something is brewing deep inside you, when life has been full throttle and you're feeling a bit wilted, not sure what the fuck happened, because you did everything you were supposed to, but it seems life came in matt instead of sheen. And that is why you picked up this book.

Either way, in the pages that follow, I will show you how to answer the right question.

We spend the early part of our lives asking what we want our lives to look like. We create a vision, Pinterest optional, of all the boxes we want to tick to build the structure from which our lives will seamlessly hang, no ironing required. We pick up cultural cues, parental influence and expectations, educational steers, belief systems and behavioural patterns and use them to draw a road map, ticking boxes along the way, trying to paint the picture of how we want our life to look like as we go. Some of those boxes may include some, or all, from the prescribed Successful Life Checklist:

- ★ Education
- ★ Travel
- ★ Career ladder
- ★ Partner
- ★ House
- ★ Family
- ★ Decent bra

For women, this is also stapled to the Wonder Woman To-Do List:

- ★ Be beautiful, be perfect (but make it seem effortless)
- ★ Be ballsy (but never angry – no, anger is not an accessory that looks good on women)
- ★ Be clever (but not too clever, especially in certain company)
- ★ Be feminine and nurturing (but clip the feminine faults of being too emotional, too soft, too flirty, too frigid)
- ★ Break glass ceilings (but make sure you clean up the mess).

So you check the boxes and now stand completely frazzled, wondering why there isn't a Welcome Cocktail, because surely you've 'Arrived!' But all you feel is knackered. Utterly exhausted. Afraid. Bored. Frustrated. Underwhelmed. Overwhelmed. Or any mash up of these.

There is no midlife crisis. (Partly because the dinner needs to be made, you don't have time.) The term was coined in 1965 by psychoanalyst Elliott Jaques, but subsequent research has debunked it. There is, however, a midlife slump that occurs when your expectations have hit the intersection with reality. There is a U-shaped happiness curve that shows our happiness in youth dips in mid-age and grows again in later years. Most research has focused on men (quelle surprise!) but thankfully women are gradually being seen as people in their own right and the impact of enormous changes relating to menopause and roles as mothers are now being researched. We are now younger for longer, so this brief slump is actually a good thing. This is the opportunity you've been waiting for. Trust me. That feeling means something has jolted you out of autopilot and now you get to press pause, and reflect. Now is the time to ask the right question.

Not, what do I want my life to look like?
But what do I want my life to *feel* like?

Why this midlife is unique

For something that labels many of us, defining midlife today is surprisingly difficult. The term still hankers to an outdated vision of a disappearing woman who has outgrown her sexuality, use and status. Yet you are very much here, thank you very much, bursting with desires and ambitions but often not quite knowing what to do with them. That's because none of the standard rules about age – and mid-age – apply anymore.

You may or may not have realised this, but you are part of the generation of women who are redefining midlife.

There has *never* been a midlife like this one.

Firstly, we've been gifted an extra twenty or thirty years of life expectancy. To put this in context, when my mum Pat was born in 1934, her life expectancy at birth was fifty-nine. That's not a typo. Fifty-nine. Now, because of incredible advancements in healthcare over the last century, she was, in fact, eighty-three when she died. When I was born in 1970, my life expectancy was seventy-four – already fifteen years more than my mum, and I'm likely to live much longer. When my last daughter Ruby was born in 2010 her life expectancy at birth was eighty-three (likely to be adjusted to 100).

So between my mum and daughter, there is more than twenty-five years of extra living.

But that's not what makes this time so special. What makes this generation so unique is that these extra decades are to be lived in the middle of your life, not the end.

In midlife, not in old age.

And here's why. We have unprecedented freedoms and opportunities that no generations of women in history have experienced: financial, educational, academic, career, travel, sports and leisure. Potentially we have more than two extra midlife decades, along with choices and chances that women before us could only have dreamed of. But what makes it so utterly unique, is that women like you and me now get to have a decades-long stage of life before old age, that is not centred around the traditional role of Breeder and Facilitator of Everyone Else's Lives. Throughout history, women have been mostly valued for, and defined by, their role as mothers and nurturers. Once this responsibility was fulfilled, they were deemed 'old' and fecked into the corner to knit, desexualised and devalued. But today, women are living a third to half our lives post-menopausal and for the FIRST TIME IN HISTORY, women have the chance to live creative, vibrant, fulfilled lives not just in relation to who we are to others, but who we are to ourselves.

We are living lives as sexual, sensual, vibrant, creative, ambitious, adventurous, skilful, educated, dynamic, loving, nurturing, valued and valuable women in our own right. For millennia, only valued as wives and mothers, today women no longer even have to have kids. Or get married. Or follow any of the cultural expectations that harnessed women into very clear roles and responsibilities. Not that there's anything wrong with those roles. They are fulfilling and valuable for those who want them. They just no longer have to be the *only* roles that give us value. Now we have at least two decades to explore a new landscape where we can be whoever, and whatever, we need and want to be.

Yet, it can also be brain-meltingly confusing. And challenging. And a little overwhelming. 'Having it all' can just feel an awful lot like doing it all. The never-ending list of things you have to do but never quite get round to hangs over you like the threat of grey roots during a global pandemic. But that's only because of the cultural hangover that your role is to be everything to everyone. It's time you put you on top of that To-Do list.

There has been a recent trend in pop psychology and clever memes about how to give *less* fucks. This book is about how to give *more* fucks. But only about you, your life and how you want it to feel. This can feel really hard. Partly because women have been so conditioned to live our lives in terms of our output to others, we can struggle to live it in terms of input to ourselves. Partly because this new midlife landscape is so virgin and the signposts so few, it can be hard to figure out which path to take. And partly because our lives are so filled with busyness and expectations to deliver, firefighting bumps on the road and trying to figure out what the hell we're supposed to be eating this year (is kale out or just hovering in the doorway, one leaf in, one leaf out, while beetroot makes a play for prominence?), we can drift through these years in a fit of fury, a slurry of sleep-deprivation, a mayhem of menopause, a ladder of standards so high we can't even see the top. We risk waking up one day having had our heads barrelled down in survival mode and not recognise the person staring back in the mirror.

Your life isn't fucking perfect, even though you did everything right! You slump back to the bedroom to patch up your disappointed face with makeup, scan the wardrobe for an outfit that isn't as tired as you, and smile/grimace into the mirror to mutter 'Let's do this,' as you take on another day like someone who's running a marathon but only got to 10km in training.

> ***You, me, and this generation of women are the first to explore the landscape that has two or three decades of extra life expectancy, to be lived in the middle of our lives, that we haven't really accounted for or mapped out.***

Yet, the landscape is unchartered and many of us don't feel we have a compass. Through the pages and exercises in this book, you will discover what an amazing opportunity you now have to trail blaze this inspiring new midlife landscape, and with curiosity, intention and a big coloured marker for those new signposts, you'll find that that compass is actually in you.

With this midlife mission in mind, it's not about changing, hiding or fighting your age; it's about recognising that your age is so different from previous generations that it is a groundbreaking age. A new age. A redefined mid-age: better, bolder, brighter.

This book is about taking the time to think. Not about the child-care cover for half-term. Not about the presentation you have to do in front of that sniggering man-child who happens to be your boss. Not about the mathematical equation you have to solve of how to collect two kids from two different schools at the same time as you have to get a corn removed because, although the heels you wore made your legs look thinner, they fucked up your feet.

This is time to think about you.
To learn. About you.
To explore. You.

It's like that age-old story that's been re-told a million times in books and romcoms. Off goes the troubled traveller to 'find themselves' in foreign lands/the arms of the right person/the Cosmo questionnaire on *Who Are You Really?* that just makes you more confused. Meanwhile, 'themselves' is lumbering after them, their permanent shadow all along. The treasure is in you. All you have to do is down domestic/societal expectations/work tools long enough to open the damn box. You think you can only get that perfect facial glow from the latest overpriced filter cream? But there's another way. Let the glow from the internal light of living a life you have designed reflect on your face. No makeup brand has ever managed that shade.

You are likely mid-flow in midlife. It's time to press Refresh to assess the messy mayhem of your life, having possibly accumulated partners, marriages, divorces, children being born, children being raised, children leaving home, parent care, parent loss, career building, career stagnation, redundancy, change of direction, change of pace, change thrust upon you, change created by you, unexpected outcomes, disappointments, disillusion, wine bellies, unwanted chin hairs, and opportunities, passions and ambitions.

As little girls, we all had dreams. Midlife is the time to make sure those dreams, if they haven't been achieved already, don't get lost in nostalgia and dirty dishes. It's time to stop always asking what do I want my life to look like (and does my bum look big in it?) and explore how you want your life to feel like, and then start writing the signposts.

I believe we don't just have an opportunity. We also have a responsibility. We are the bridge between the generations before and the generations to come. You and me are the trailblazers. We have to role model a new way for women to live; we have to write these new signposts for these new decades of vibrant, valuable, creative, inspired, fulfilled midlife living. We bridge from the generations who couldn't do or have what we can do and have. I think of the countless women who signed their works 'Anonymous'. I think of the countless women who died because of their gall to be outspoken. I think of the generations of women whose scope was limited by societal expectation and legislated restriction; the women who had to give up work when they married, who had passions and skills and talent but denied a place at the table in academia, science, medicine, politics, business, literature, art, music. All that wasted potential.

But we also need to show my daughters, and your daughters, and the next generation that the only way for women to be successful is not to always be living under a cloud of overwhelm; to always be putting everyone else's needs first; to be constantly busy, struggling to juggle, being pulled in every direction, being so many things to so many people we've no idea who we are to ourselves.

We get to change that model. You get to change that model.

We have a responsibility to tread new paths and take advantage of this extraordinary time we've been given to show that women can forge ahead to function as human beings, not just human doings.

Finding your purpose

You hear so much these days about finding your purpose.

Well, I believe that your first and foremost purpose in life is you.

And from that place of strength, everyone, and everything, in your life will benefit.

When I coach women, the hardest part for them is often realising they have to write their own permission slip. No one else is going to do it for you ('what's new?', says you.) This doesn't mean you have to blow up your current life, or stop loving and nurturing your family and friends. It simply means that this is your time to empower yourself to put you on the To-Do list. Not at the bottom, or in the middle, but at the top. I know that this idea may feel risky and subverted – that you might put yourself first. That's only because the cultural matrix you've grown up in has told women for millennia that they can only have value by giving to others. They never had this time to, in a sense, give birth back to themselves after perhaps birthing a family.

Through this book you are first going on a mission of self-discovery, exploring you. Then you are going to start designing a life based on how you want it to feel. And finally you are going to take action and start living more intentionally. I'll be guiding you at every stage, partly through my experience coaching women like you, and through my own experience going through all of these changes and choices myself. You'll be doing the work, but I'll be poking you with a stick. Sorry, but that's just the way it is. You don't hire a personal trainer and then expect them to do the heavy lifting for you (unless he's gorgeous and you've asked him round to move your bedroom furniture).

I'm not just talking the talk. I have walked the talk

I sprang into my adult life with enthusiasm and a backpack, eager to leave behind a childhood where, growing up in the Troubled seventies and eighties of Belfast, I'd been given very clear instructions on who I could be and which side of the fence I should sit. I travelled, I studied, I travelled some more, building up boyfriends, qualifications and a penchant for partying like many young people my age. I then followed the prescribed script of getting the 'serious' job, buying an apartment, and swapping boyfriends for a husband. Before I knew it, I was a home owner, married and pregnant (in the space of six months as it happened). The next decade was a whirl of trying for babies, losing babies, having babies, dinner parties, career switches, laughing, crying, sleep deprivation, holidays, and all the ingredients that make up what becomes a midlife of mayhem. I thought it was normal to feel overworked, overstretched and overwhelmed. Wasn't I living the dream? That women could finally have it all? In this life feeling frantically rushed, I frantically shushed the little voice inside that whispered 'Why does this feel so wrong?'

And then it all came crashing down. Four days after my third baby Ruby was born, my beautiful, loving mum had a catastrophic stroke. She was left paralysed apart from her left arm, and brain damaged. She would never say my name again. I would spend the following months spoon-feeding and changing them both, and the next five years sandwiched between child-care and parent-care. In my book *The Sandwich Years*, I explain what happens when in the midst of that, you forget about self-care. During this time, my marriage was in free fall, and eventually ended. I was suddenly thrust into the singular hell that is single parenting. And less than a year later, my lovely mum died in my arms.

And that's where I start this book: standing in the rubble of a life I had known, my marriage over, my mother dead after five years of being sandwiched between caring for her and small children, my career on life support, and mid-aged. Yes, without me realising, I had ploughed through a decade with my head bent in utter survival mode, shocked to realise I was 'technically' middle aged! It felt like my entire sense of identity had been washed away with the thousands of laundry loads.

I write this book, not just as a qualified life and leadership coach now who works as The MidLife Coach with women who want to not only navigate midlife but kick ass in it too, but also as a woman who reached middle age not recognising the grey-rooted reflection looking back in the mirror. I will share my own journey of discovery as I encourage and guide you to not only see the woman in the mirror, but to hear her too. Just like I had to learn how to sign my own permission slip to start redefining and redesigning my life, I will coach you on how to design a bespoke midlife just for you.

Midlife is a time to reform based on your own values, strengths, desires, and design. It doesn't mean you have to blow up your current life (unless you want to). Nor does it mean it needs to be blown up in order to redesign your life based on what you want, not what is expected of you. I had to re-learn who I was, something many of us actually never take the time to do. Like I will show you how to do in this book, I had to accept change and discover who I was, recognise I had choices and start designing a life that I wanted to live, finding clarity to deliver on the potential my life has to offer. I'm going to tell you some wonderful stories of women just like you, women I have coached who went about figuring out who they were again, and often surprising even themselves.

This is the best time of my life – not because life is perfect and I've discovered calorie-free wine, but because I have learned how to live with intention, adapting to change, making choices, and moving with clarity.

Warning: I swear. Not a lot, but occasionally. This book is about being you. So swearing is me. It doesn't make me big or clever. It just makes me me. If you're offended by swear words, just read something else. Sugar. Feck. Fudge. Bottom. Whatever tickles your fancy. Let me be me, and you be you. No one is right and no one is wrong. But if one message comes through this book it is that I will no longer pretend to be anything other than who I am. And I want that for you. So let me swear, and you read something else, and then we can get on with the essence of this book … striding out in your Docs/heels/

sandals/runners/sensible shoes with a instep/frivolous shoes and a blister plaster – taking the steps forward, leaving your footprints in the sand, not following anyone else's. Making this unique midlife, uniquely yours.

You can download many of the exercises in these chapters from www.themidlifecoach.org/midliferedefined/resources. Please use the Code MYMIDLIFE to access the resources and templates.

SECTION 1:
Self-discovery

★

WHO AM I AND HOW DID *I Get Here?*

★

In many ways, perhaps I was lucky. Change didn't just creep up on me like a waiter constantly filling your wine glass without you noticing, so you've no idea how drunk you are until you stand up and wonder why the floor has risen so fast to meet you. Change rang the bell and when I opened the door, a wrecking ball smashed through and demolished the life I knew. Within the space of a year my marriage ended and my mum died.

Being afflicted by the double whammy of Good Girl Conditioning and Perfectionism, this seemingly careless multiple loss was crippling to me. I was not a woman who flounders. No. I was a woman who does, and delivers, and does some more. Yet here I was flailing, untethered, cast adrift in unchartered waters. The two most significant structures in my life – the family I was born into, and the family I had created – were dismantled without planning permission, leaving me in my mid-forties floundering like a beached whale. This, at the end of an exhausting decade of trying for babies, losing babies, having babies, raising three beautiful babies, giving up a career that had defined me, figuring out a new one that allowed me to work, think and change nappies; a decade where I spent half of it sandwiched between caring for young children and a mum who required twenty-four- hour care.

I was barely drawing breath, never mind putting actual thought into my life other than could I get through the day on three gins or less, and 'is it bedtime yet?' I bounced from care need to care need – my children, my mum, my career, my marriage, my family, my friends – with no care left for my care needs. I had lost all sense of myself as a person.

It wasn't just the external things that were changing. My body was also doing things I didn't want it to. Like someone with physical Tourettes, my body was exploding randomly with socially embarrassing outbursts – a hot flush here, rampant chin hairs there, and a cacophony of mood swings so extreme I could run through a fairly impressive repertoire in sixty seconds. Except no one was impressed. My periods betrayed a lifetime of exemplary time keeping, starting to behave like twenty-first century weather forecasts now that global warming has kicked in – floods, heavy rain, and unexpected deluges. And while we're on the subject of global warming, my body's eco system switched hemisphere overnight. Then my mind began to act like a perverse sieve that lets the veg out but keeps the water in, holding useless information such as lyrics to songs I didn't sing any more, while letting go of all the stuff I needed – my children's names, my password for Netflix and on one occasion when I got on the bus, the name of the road I lived on. It wasn't all bad. I still lived a functioning life. I loved my children, had great friends, and enjoyed my burgeoning career as a copywriter and journalist. But really? Could life not stand still for one damn minute so I could catch my breath?

I always remembered entering my mum's bedroom in the days after her stroke; a bedroom she herself would never see again as we cared for her downstairs in a hastily converted dining-room to bedroom for the next five years. As I stood in the doorway, the memories of me as a child clambering onto her bed for morning cuddles seemed to reach out and embrace me like her arms used to, her smell softly soothing me; a subtle mix of clean laundry, a hint of Estée Lauder's *Beautiful* and slightly singed hair from her dangerously old curling tong. On her bedside table sat a novel, the bookmark one of my daughters had made her poking up halfway through the pages; a book she would never now finish. Makeup was scattered on the dressing table: makeup I would now have to apply for her. The outfit she had left out to wear for lunch with her friend the day after she returned from helping me after Ruby was born, hanging on the wardrobe handle; clothes she would never wear again, her wardrobe now reduced to bed wear and easily fitting clothes. Her bedroom that day showed a life in motion, of plans being made, drenched in nostalgia with photos of me, my brother, and her grandchildren; a life in full flow. Downstairs, my mum – my kind, loving, generous, social, couldn't-let-me-walk-past-without-reaching-out-to-touch-my-arm-or-stroke-my-hair mum was gone, replaced by someone who could barely reach for her own hair.

I had stared at her half-finished book, the abandoned makeup and left-out clothes and realised for perhaps the first time in my own mile-a-minute life, how fragile and transient it all actually is. The next few years I just kept my head down trying to survive the days. They were tough beyond my wildest nightmares. Marriage disintegrating and the toll of helping my dad care for Mum, while trying to work and raise three feisty girls alone, meant I was more often than not overwhelmed, constantly stretched and constantly feeling a failure. The only thing I excelled at was guilt. Because like many women, I was conditioned to believe I was never doing enough, constantly reacting, never getting in front of anything to be able to think it out, or create a space to breathe, always leaping from one burning fire to another. Over the next few years, that stark shock of her bedroom that day stayed with me, like a bookmark following me on the pages of my days, reminding me that my own life was fragile and transient.

None of us knows what lies ahead. It took me a long time to emerge from the changes and circumstances of my life to understand that I could still direct it. The problem was I was so used to autopilot survival mode, I wasn't sure I could remember how to fly. I knew I was flailing, untethered, but I just kept hoping the Charlotte Tilsbury Hollywood Filter was filtering out the imperfections of my life.

Outward appearance: perfectionism, 'fine', functioning.
Inward reality: turmoil, terror, rudderless.

I realised I'd forgotten who I was. I knew *what* I was: an exhausted firefighting ninja. I knew *how* I was; a tornado of anger, grief, confusion, fear and perfectionist pressure. I knew *where* I was;

in murky waters called middle age, with no life-jacket, no map and no plan. I had to learn to live all over again, not in a skin lifted off the rack, but in my own skin. Five years later, as The MidLife Coach using my own experiences and extensive training, I empower women to deal with the changes that can happen at this exciting and challenging time of life, and find the potential in their lives. Today, not when the dishes are done and curvier figures are back in fashion. Today.

We are conditioned to believe happiness is the only state we should be in, otherwise we are a failure. Yet few of us are happy 100% of the time (those that are either have an intravenous gin drip, or live in an alternate universe). So this might come as a shock.

Genuine, Not Fake News Flash: It's not normal to be happy all the time. It's normal to have a wide range of positive and negative emotions, sometimes all in the space of three minutes. We have been conditioned to view some feelings as good, and some as bad, making us feel uncomfortable when we have them. But we're not bad or mad to be angry, or deflated or tense. These are genuine feelings that when listened to, teach us about ourselves, so we can then choose how to respond to the reason, not the feeling. Listen with both ears that is, not just half an ear while half is listening for the sound of the washing machine cycle to finish and the other one is trying to juggle the baying demands from a variety of people, animals and fitbit notifications urgently reminding you that you haven't met your target number of steps.

That's why the first section of this book is all about audits. As you look at the impact of change, and how to deal with it, please just be open to the idea of discomfort becoming your new pet as you try to sit with it, even when it's peeing on the carpet.

You want to find the magic in midlife despite, because and including all the changes that are happening, to realise you have the power to also action change. Change happens because of natural circumstances – children appearing in our lives, children leaving home, menopause. Other times, change is thrust upon us – job losses, divorce, bereavement, illness and changes you choose to make. Focusing on what life should look like, you can lurch from change to change without focusing on what you really want your life to feel like.

Just like you inevitably need glasses as you age, sometimes you need glasses for your mind – to see more clearly where you are going.

In this section you're going to put on those glasses and look at how change is affecting you, what changes are happening, and carry out an audit of your life, your body, your values and strengths so you can venture forwards with a fully stocked backpack and an emergency bar of chocolate. Discovery isn't just about rediscovering who you were, but who you are now with all the experiences, mistakes, lessons, learnings, inspirations, revelations, pain and gain.

If it feels risky doing audits, I promise you, taking stock is like pulling out everything in your underwear drawer and deciding what you need to throw out, what still fits and looks great, and where are the gaps – do you need something sexy, something flattering, or just a bright new colour? So that when you put everything back in, you know that every piece has a place. Let's go rummage in your drawers.

1

WHAT THE *Actual Fuck?*

★

WHERE AM I?

The spray of vomit fanned out like a dragon's fire-fuelled breath, engulfing two racks of M&S work trousers, with a splattering of undigested diced carrot reaching a perfectly poised mannequin. This spew of lunch was sharply accompanied by a communal intake of breaths just before a shriek of despair as my two-year-old daughter Daisy turned in her double buggy and threw up again, this time all over her one-year-old sister Poppy. Like a grown-up child, I spun round to my mum, expecting – hoping – she would make it all go away. Instead I saw that she too had the look of a woman about to disown her daughter and run to the knickers department pretending she was looking for a thermal vest. Twenty minutes later, having used up an industrial roll of blue tissue, and apologising 372 times to the extremely lovely staff who had valiantly picked pieces of carrot off the now disrobed mannequin whilst shrilling. 'It's absolutely fine, don't be worrying about it,' I pushed the double buggy into the toilets, already defeated by the day despite it only being 9.38am. I relieved both my children of their sick-sodden clothes, hoping my mum hurried back soon with clean replacements. I knew this was futile though, because once she started looking at outfits for her grandchildren, she'd be lost in a fug of motherly nostalgia. Then my phone rang.

'Fuck! Fuckedy fuck,' I grimaced, noticing the ludicrously long and foreign number. A work call. *That* work call. 'Fuckedy fuck!' squealed my deliriously-happy-now-she'd-been-sick child.

'Fuck. Don't say that!' I simpered as I had no choice but to accept the call from a doctor in Congo dealing with the Ebola crisis. When I'd arranged the call of course, I wasn't meant to be in a toilet with two vomit-clad children and my mother. I was meant to have nimbly navigated my 'dependents' into the M&S cafe, bought them snacks and then gone to hide in the unpopular, and therefore quiet, men's V-neck section to take the call so that when I got home and co-ordinated the kids' naps, I could pretend to be part of the adult working world, fulfilling my job as a freelance campaign writer for the non-profit sector. Like most scenarios in this ridiculous life I found myself in, I struggled through the interview with one hand taking notes, while the other pressed a finger to my mouth, eyes screaming silent 'Shushes' to my girls, and did the best I could. Just as the call ended, Mum returned with wholly inappropriate, non-emergency-replacement clothes that were wasted on the sick-scented bodies of my babies. Later that night, as I chugged a G&T, I probably laughed, slightly hysterically, about it all, making light of the carnage of managing parenting, daughtering, working, and generally coping. Sure, that's just what we do, isn't it? Accepting this pace of life as the price to pay for being able to 'have it all'. Quelling the queasy voice inside that is trying to articulate that the price feels too high, but ashamed to let the words form because so many before us never had this chance.

There have been so many days when my brain felt it had too many tabs open. Yet I needed them there. They made me feel valuable and busy, and you know, moving. Because if I stopped, well then thoughts would appear, and who the hell wants to be confronted with the neurotic, hormone-ravaged thoughts of a woman on the verge of another meltdown? Whenever my laptop would quit unexpectedly, fusing with the fury of never being turned off, I'd be panic punched, wondering if all the Chrome tabs of ideas, thoughts and stuff to learn/do/figure out that were holding my life together would be lost in the ethereal; that place who will paint dip my furniture, the Guardian article on how to have better sex despite no sleep, the online journal for the thoughts I was too scared to write down, the work related tabs, the personal related tabs, the aspirational tabs, the practical tabs. Yet for a micro-moment when I restarted my computer, the Chrome page opening up fresh and blank, it felt like a new beginning, and I could just for a few silly seconds imagine having NO TABS OPEN. But before my nervous system could explore this subverted idea, my mouse moved automatically to Browser History, returning them as quickly as possible, lest the ground started to shake and the walls of my life cracked open. The lists were reinstated. The Pressure. The Business. The Busyness. The Responsibility. Why? The F word. Fear. Fear of not being perfect. Fear of not being in control. Fear of not pleasing everyone. Fear of dropping balls, but there were so many damn balls, I only had two arms, but there were just so many damn balls. Quick! Open a new tab: 'How to keep juggling balls without your head exploding?'

There is a voice of longing inside every woman. 'Let me out,' it whispers behind the scenes as we perform in so many ways to so many people. It screams louder in the silence of night as we struggle to sleep because in being so many things to so many people, we're forgetting what we are to ourselves. We are so intent on being great mothers, lovers, friends, we never think to be all of those things to ourselves. It begins with being told to be a Good Girl and then bullies us into adulthood. We strive to be perfect versions of an expected ideal: good partners, good daughters, mothers, bosses, colleagues, friends, neighbours. We somehow hope all this striving will make us feel alive. Often though, we are just left feeling weary. Lost. Overwhelmed. We look at all the energy we output, and can't help wondering why it doesn't feel more fulfilling.

Carrying Extra Weight

Most women carry extra weight. I'm not referring to the wine belly. I mean the obese weight of the emotional burden we bear, trying to make everyone else's life work, as well as everything in our own lives – our partners, our parents, our children, our colleagues, our friends, our homes, our bodies, our work places, our community. The blossoming of breasts appears to miraculously pre-condition us into believing we are responsible for everyone else's happiness; nurturers who must say yes to everyone else's needs. E-V-E-R-Y-ONE else's. Isn't it a shame we aren't taught how to include our own happiness on this list? It's not just the emotional burden. Although we live with a new generation of men who (mostly) know how to work the washing machine, can cook, change nappies, and (mostly) understand that sex is much better if the woman actually enjoys it, it is still a fact that women carry the heavier laundry load, despite the fact that we are often *also* now working. We bring home some of the bacon, still fry it, and then scrub the fatty frying pan. In the 2019 Gender Equality Index, the gap was smallest in that virtuous country Sweden, where 56 per cent of men and 74 per cent of women undertook housework every day, which is still a significant gap. In Ireland, while men did more housework in 2019 than in 2005, women did too while also taking up more space in the workforce, and so the gap between them remains at 40 per cent. In the UK that gap is 60 per cent. This isn't about blame per se, but about acknowledging every one of those balls you juggle and struggle to keep in the air. Acknowledging you aren't failing, but flailing.

My to-do lists had to-do lists – with their own little network going on, like busy ants, multiplying and feeding off each other. I thought I could survive the mayhem with a sturdy supply of colour coded post-it notes, washable pens and four hours' sleep a night. I was wrong. Three children under five, a husband who worked long hours and then left, a mother who needed twenty-four hour care, a career that needed surgery – it was carnage. Proper *Grey's Anatomy* – there has been an earthquake, a power cut, AND a knife-wielding murderer on the loose – carnage. I needed a crash cart on standby most days. It felt like I had entered a wind tunnel by accident and couldn't find the way out, my jowls flapping in the gusts, my hair blowing in a not-like-in-the-movies-sexy-but-like-a-wild-witch-having-a-bad-hair-day-way. All those sign posts I had followed and this is where they had led me?

And while my circumstances were unique to me, the feelings of total overwhelm and loss of control are not. Covid-19 aside, stress is the new Plague. The World Health Organization has called stress the health epidemic of the twent-first century. Balance (or finding it) is the new religion.

Meabh is a client of mine in her late fifties. When I asked her recently how she had spent her Sunday, she told me she'd actually had a rare day to herself. But she didn't know what to do with the time, so she did all the ironing and then caught up on work for the rest of the day. She's been so busy for so long, looking after so many responsibilities, she has no idea how to rest.

There is nothing more stressful, however, than being told stress is bad for you when you're up to your (unshaped) eyebrows with the stuff. There is nothing more likely to send you off kilter than to be told you have to find balance. We know all the things we are supposed to do, but we're too stressed and unbalanced to get round to doing any of them. The de-stressing activities just cause more stress because *we can't fit them in!*

Overwhelm is often driven by our *expectations*, not the actual tasks we have to do. Expectations like:

★ If everyone around me isn't happy, it's my fault. Must try harder.

★ It's imperative I keep my house clean and tidy or I will look like a failure. And they'll do a TV show on me, and no one will be my friend, even though I'm generous and kind and really good fun after two gins.

★ If I drop a ball, I must be really bad at organisation/time planning/everything. Do more. Get up earlier.

★ I have to leave for that appointment, but I've the washing to put on or else the whole family structure will fall apart and I will have to wear a sackcloth (will it make my bum look big?) and a plaque around my neck saying 'Good Girl? Ha! Good for Nothing, more like'

★ I feel so guilty for shouting at my children but please, can someone just agree with me that they can be REALLY

UNREASONABLE! I know we're not supposed to complain about being a mother, but FUCK it's hard!

- ★ Sorry, sorry. I shouldn't have said/thought/felt that. Sorry. I'm really fine. Sorry. Yes, totally fine. Sorry.
- ★ Ah, posting my pic of my kids dressed up for Halloween to show I'm a decent parent. Wait, why do mine look so pathetic and shop bought? Oh my God, did Sinead actually make that outfit? It's amazing. Crap. How can I delete my photo? It's not good enough. I'M NOT GOOD ENOUGH!

As my husband packed the spare wine glasses into the back of his car, along with the life I was living, apart from asking the obvious question – what the hell just happened? – I had to ask the scarier question – what do I do now? And how can I possibly manage to juggle any more balls? (The Guinness World Record is eleven balls. Pah! Most women could do that in their sleep).

Mayhem is a midlife monster we need to tame. Mayhem clouds our focus, it distorts our sight, and it drains our energy.

> ***Living in mayhem means it is far too easy, and way too common, for women to drift into, and out the other side of midlife, without really taking any conscious intentional path.***

We might hit that well-used phrase – midlife crisis. But really it's a wake-up call that we don't have to accept this paradigm that the madness of mayhem is the only way to live successfully. To challenge the lie we've been sold that this is our lot. That we *can* stop living in mayhem, that we *can* put our own happiness on the to-do list, and use this time as an opportunity to make decisions that serve us well.

Audit #1 – Your life balance

Imagine you're standing in the middle of your life as it plays out around you. You look one way and can see to a certain point in the distance, and a width of range across you. There are blindspots however, and your horizon is limited by your position. Now imagine you get in a helicopter and hover above this midpoint. You can now look down and see your whole life from one viewpoint. Well, buckle up, you're taking off.

This exercise is called the Wheel of Life. It sounds like a TV gameshow, and you might even find there are some million-dollar questions to answer, but being honest about your current situation is key – deciding on a score that is real, rather than aspirational. This is about doing a quick audit to see where you are right now, at this moment in your life. Either download the Wheel of Life template from my website www.themidlifecoach.org/MidlifeRedefinedResources, or draw a large circle on a sheet of paper or notebook. Draw a line down the middle, across the middle and split those quadrants so that you end up with a wheel with eight spokes.

I'm going to suggest eight headings for each of those segments, but this is *your* life, so if you want to change or split any of them, please do. This Wheel has to represent the elements of your life.

- ★ Career/job
- ★ Money/finance
- ★ Health
- ★ Significant relationship/romance
- ★ Family and friends
- ★ Hobbies/passions/leisure/fun
- ★ Spiritual/personal growth/learning
- ★ Physical environment (you could even split this if you like into commute and home environment)

You could replace some of those with:

- ★ Social life
- ★ Belonging in community
- ★ Personal space
- ★ Fitness
- ★ Travel
- ★ Sex
- ★ Food/diet
- ★ Mental health/emotional wellbeing

Once you have your Wheel and headings, imagining the centre is zero, and the outer edge is 10, start marking each section according to how you would rate them right now, on a scale of 1–10, with 1 being very low and 10 being very high. Draw a line in an arc across that section from one side to the other. Take your time and really think about each section. DO NOT WORRY about the scores – no one is watching you and your life is not to be compared to someone else's. This is not a self-flagellation game. It's an audit. All you are doing is taking a helicopter view of your life, so you can decide where, if anywhere, you would like to redress an imbalance, invest more energy or make some changes.

This is Orientation 101: in order to figure out where you want to go, you have to know where you are.

When you are done, you will have a sort of spider web and unless you mark every section the same number which is unlikely, it will look higgledy-piggledy. Maybe one section is an eight, while the next is a three, and the one beside that is a five.

How does it look to you? Balanced? Surprising? What you expected? All you need to do for now is just accept it as it is and reflect on the scores that are lower. (We'll be using it later in Section 2). Remember, at a particular point in your life, you may want or need to be focusing more energy on different aspects. Balance isn't necessarily having everything the same number. Balance – at this time of your life – is whatever you need it to be. You may have invested more time in your career, but now need to look more at Fun & Leisure. This Wheel is about giving you perspective to allow you to make adjustments if you want to, and to see what areas need a little investment of your time and energy.

Now pick a couple of sections with lower scores and think about one small action that would take it up a number. So maybe under Signifiant Other, to move that from a four to a five might be as simple as deciding to put a date in the diary once a month to have a date/no TV night/TV night. Just having it in the diary is one step better than constantly saying 'We must try and have some quality time.' Under Hobbies, to move it from a six to a seven it might be signing up for some golf lessons, or emailing that group of friends to do that spa weekend you've been harping on about for three years. Look at each number, and ask what one small action would it take to increase that number by one.

Well done. Life audit complete. Information is power, and by the end of this section, you're going to know just how much juice you have in your charger pack.

2

CAN I NOT AGE ANY *Damn Way I Want?*

★

HOW AM I?

Ageing was definitely not on my to-do list.

Travelling: tick.

Learning: tick.

Having fun: tick.

Ageing: not so much.

Yet ageing is happening anyway because, well, it's biology. I do wonder why we suddenly associate ageing as being from thirty-five or forty? I've been ageing since the day I was born, so why did it suddenly become such a thing? Perhaps we all have that moment. That seismic shift when we decide we're no longer part of the youth culture, because our culture is now playing out on Radio Gold. Maybe it's that sucker punch when we realise that the beautiful arrogance of 'it all being ahead of us' is looking a tad fragile as we look over our shoulder and see a crumpled face lying on the ground

– like a snake, we've just shed our taut skin. Perhaps it's when we realise our definition of a good night out has changed: we used to measure it by the time we got home, the later after midnight the better. Now we still measure it by the time we get home: if we get in before midnight, AND hang our clothes up, it's a winner. My moment came when I saw my mum's unfinished book and realised my life wasn't a practice run. I want to make sure I have lived long and well enough to figure out what golden nuggets of wisdom I will tell my children on my deathbed. I'm not sure 'wash your draining board out occasionally or else it will smell' feels like a deep enough legacy.

Is it when our hand hovers in the chemist, about to reach for the same face cream we've always used, but now hesitate, bewildered and bothered by the branding screaming at us from every shelf: ANTI-AGEING CREAM – Buy it or shrivel up in a sucking vortex of wrinkles and folds like a pug puppy's face! But how am I supposed to anti-age? Ageing is as fundamental to living as breathing. For me, it was also a culmination of realising my body was racing ahead of my mind. In my head, I'm thirty-two. Imagine the confusion of looking at skin that's absorbed more sun than moisturiser, of muscles that have watched more Netflix than pilates instructors; of eyes that squint to read labels. I'm a positive person on the whole. But I still felt it. That slight feeling of being let down; a feeling that somehow I wasn't as attractive, interesting, or dynamic as I was when I was 'younger', yet knowing these standards haven't been set by me, are not based on truth, fact, or reason, but by a male-maintained societal airbrushed line in the sands of time.

Smart and rational as I was, I was also battered and bruised, and so allowed myself to be swayed by the branding, marketing and TV ads that perpetuate a myth that youth is best. Which made me, what? Second best? Worst? Last? I succumbed and grabbed the overly priced anti-ageing cream, loathing myself as much as my skin.

We all know anti-ageing propaganda is Fake News, but we are forced to pander to its petulance anyway. We are bullied by the manipulative messaging that serves no one except the beauty industry, magazine sales and the comfortable shoe market. Ageing is not a disease. It's not even a condition like bad breath that you can mask with a mint. Ageing is not one of those fashion trends that just doesn't suit you, like thongs and culottes, no matter how many times they try to come back.

> ***Ageing is a fucking privilege, yet we're made to feel grateful for still being allowed out in public.***

Getting sucked into the anti-ageing movement is like joining the Mean Girls – we feel pressured to join, we feel we're fitting in, but we know it's not right; morally, authentically, emotionally. Ageing is normal, yet somehow it has become de-normalised. It's something natural and important, and yet everywhere we turn we are being told not to do it. What women actually need is to be left alone by the Society Stasi who constantly judge women on how they look, and how they make themselves feel and look good. Botox and filler? Letting hair go grey? Dyeing it? Sheering it short, letting it grow? Expensive face creams or soap and water? Skin plumping procedures or fucking face yoga? It's no one's business but yours what you do, or why you do it. But the pressure to please some fake ideal that youth is best needs to stop, and we are the only ones who can. When I mentioned to a much younger friend about discovering a white pubic hair, she recoiled in horror as if I'd told her I had Ebola, as if ageing was an infectious disease, instead of hopefully something we will all get. I know enough people who never made it far enough to get a white pubic hair. Ageing as a negative notion is simply a destructive marketing construct.

> ***Ageing as a reality is a natural process that, like youth, has opportunities, challenges, highs, lows, benefits, contradictions, fear, joy, good days and bad days.***

Ageing is a natural process. However, like a compliment that actually hides an insult, the scourge of Anti-Ageing Propaganda has made women feel hopeful and humiliated at the same time. Even the pseudo-posturing that forty is the new thirty, and fifty is the new twenty, still advocates that being younger is better, while trying to suggest you can still be relevant DESPITE your age. Youth is not better. Who the hell wants to grow up in the selfie generation? Here's what you have to realise.

> *Forty is the NEW forty … redefined, reformed and redesigned. By you.*
>
> *Fifty is the MOST BEAUTIFUL fifty it has ever been for women. And we have the maintenance bills to prove it (and don't care).*
>
> *Sixty is the BEST sixty in history. Literally. Not even a hundred years ago, life expectancy for women was 57.9.*
>
> *Seventy is the SEXIEST seventy that has ever gone before.*

Menopausal madness

One of the biggest disservices to women has been the shocking lack of information and support around their natural biological evolution. Even now, my teenage daughters are not being taught about menopause in their sex education and biology lessons, again reinforcing the age-old narrative that women only exist as reproductive organs. Yet women are now living a third to even half their lives post-menopausal. Regardless of what stage you are at – nowhere near it, in the middle or out the other side – knowing what your body will, is or has gone through means you can take charge of change, and focus on what to spend your money on after you've finished with the monthly monetary output for pads, tampons and nurofen. I suggest gin, but that's just me.

The year following the end of my marriage, I was so run down, stressed and scared, I was constantly sick. This included a six-week chest infection, two underarm abscesses, several colds, and a seven-month bout of insomnia. So it took me a while to realise that there were also significant changes happening that weren't just an SOS from my body to crawl into a cave and sleep for six months. My whole eco-system was changing – my metabolism, appetite, energy levels, hair growth, joint flexibility, libido, and emotional response mechanism. Added to the fact that my mum died, I had to adjust to being a single woman, a single parent while single-handedly morphing into a different body. It felt that every damn thing, except the fact that Amazon still sent my orders in inexplicably oversized packaging, was changing. My waist went missing along with some of the furniture, but I'm pretty sure my ex hadn't taken it. I learned the hard way that I should go to the loo before joining my daughter on the trampoline. My eyesight diminished as if to say, 'I can't see the future clearly anymore', metaphorically as well as physically.

Just like adolescence and youth, mid-age (or middlescence as it might be referred to) can be really confusing, partly because it also affects your brain. I lost whole chunks of knowledge, words springing just out of reach, mid-sentence. I'd never been great with names of places, people, or products with more than two syllables, so with my vocabulary now in recession I could barely communicate.

My body now has a completely different ecosystem than it had ten years ago. It was like changing from those old Economy 7 heating systems, where no matter how high you turned up the damn radiator it never got real heat, to a gas-fired central heating system. I'm not talking about menopausal hot flushes here – I mean my whole thermostat. So in addition, the flushes felt like while the gas-fired central heating was on full blast, I would occasionally (and without warning) step into a small room with a large, roaring wood-burning stove. For most of my adult life, I had worn layers and thermals, socks over tights and tights under trousers, vests and gloves. Now? I am a tropical island ... all heat and hurricanes (with the occasional emergency cocktail). My thermals, vests and layers lie derelict and defunct, my drawers springy with light-weight T-shirts and flimsy tops. I suddenly couldn't bear the feel of wool against my skin. Once a staple wardrobe fabric, if I so much as see a sheep in a field, I get a hot flush. Only cotton, flimsy, and loose clothing will suffice. I used to sleep under a 16.5 tog duvet in pyjamas (sometimes with a vest), socks, an electric blanket and occasionally a hot water bottle. Now I start with shorts and cotton vest top, and often end up naked, my legs hanging out from a 4 tog duvet.

There is a great quote from, ah you know the guy, whatshisname, you know the one, who started that Virgin business, owns an island and smiles a lot? Anyway, him. He says the most important skill of business is adaptability, but it applies to life as well. Adaptability is a vital skill for living a life where you don't end up sitting in a corner, blubbering, wishing a grown up would come along and make it all better. It came as a shock to realise I am the grown up, and all I can do is adapt or spontaneously combust.

Growing up and hitting the mid section of life is a bit like that TV show, *Changing Rooms*. You go out for milk and when you come back, your house has changed. Except it's your body. Just when you get used to waking up to discover your chin looks like a pin cushion with white (WHITE!) tough hairs, and you figure out how to add spotting and removing them to your ever growing maintenance routine, you wake up to find a forest of black (BLACK!) hair has swept over your upper lip like a field of barley swaying in the wind. Oh Richard Branson! That's yer man! The Virgin one. I knew it would come to me eventually.

Our body, our metabolism, our mind, our brain, our hormones, our perceived visibility, our ambitions, our status, our circumstances are all in a constant state of flux. Instead of 'arriving' we can't tell if we are coming or going. I love my new menopause-induced belly. No woman ever said. Middle aged spread – it's a fucking thing. We beat ourselves up that we're eating too much, drinking too much, not exercising enough and while all of these things may or may not be true, once we reach a certain age, our body (without permission, thank you very much) decides to do things differently. Ageing is a dictatorship, not a democracy. Just like that, it starts storing fat in a different part of our body, namely the front and sides. A decline in oestrogen causes cells in the abdominal area to store more fat, and may even reduce your body's ability to burn fat. So that's fact, not just fat. Except I didn't know this.

I'm a well-educated, well-informed, curious woman, and I didn't have a clue what was happening in my own body. It was only through interviewing the Director of the Dublin Well Woman clinic for a newspaper feature I was writing on menopause, I realised that some of the things happening to me could be explained by this. She told me how most of the women she sees haven't a clue what is actually happening to their bodies as they age and/or hit the peri-menopausal state. She's seen women who come to her having seen a GP worried about a heart attack because they don't understand menopause. Or women who have seen arthritis specialists because they don't understand menopause. Women just don't have the basic facts about their own bodies. Just like at school we were never taught that sex should be a pleasurable experience and not just a conduit for producing babies, we were never taught about the natural processes we will go through. Thankfully, we don't *have* to be left alone or frightened although many of us are. In my mum's generation, menopause was barely mentioned, and if it was, it was hushed and somehow shameful, like (whisper!) The Big C. How much more anxiety, fear and isolation did they suffer?

> ***Every single symptom of ageing and menopause has a natural reason, and in every single case there is something we can do about it.***

Yet often we put our own health at the bottom of the priority list. After I finished the newspaper feature, I decided that my body wasn't actually defying me in some act of rebellion. It was healthy, vibrant and progressing through a natural process that I needed to get on board with.

Once you know the facts about what is happening to you, you can do something about them. You can accept them, compensate for them, minimise symptoms, give and receive sympathy, tips and bottles of gin with fellow peri-menopausal mates, but you get to be in charge, and don't feel your body has been taken over by a megalomaniac. Which is important because after the climate change comes the flooding.

Bloody Hell

That pretty much sums up the onslaught of the peri-menopausal stage. I had been 'regular' pretty much all of my life: five days of bleeding every twenty-nine days. Suddenly my periods started trying to trick me. For three months they stopped and I thought, maybe I'm stressed? Or maybe I'm through the peri-menopause, just like that: high five, pour a gin in celebration. And just as I threw out my large period pants (you know, the ones to hold the night time pads and the heavy day dramas) my period gushed back. Literally. Gushing and goading me, flooring me with three months' worth of cramps, and, it would seem, blood. It lasted nearly two weeks. Then it stopped again, this time for four months, and as I mentally counted towards that twelve-month moment (for that is what 'menopause' is: the one day when you have had no period for twelve months. The day before that you are peri-menopausal, and the day afterwards, you are post-menopausal). But no, back it gushed, tsunami like, terrorising my life as I tried to cope with the onslaught of blood, cramps, despair and tears. My poor children were left to deal with the horror of my hormonal moods. I had two ten-day assaults in two months, and then it stopped again, retreating, leaving me terrorised and terrified of leaving the house without a baby-change bag equivalent of supplies, a paranoid wreck. My body was holding me hostage and I was reduced to whimpering to other women who were experiencing the same torment, whispering of the horror to each other in case our ovaries heard us and punished us with a three-week period. In the end, as part of my 'take charge of my life again' process, I got the coil fitted after consultation with my doctor and the Well Woman clinic. It changed everything. My periods stopped, the testosterone seemed to also balance out my moods a bit, and I could get on with the rest of the (un)bloody balls I have to juggle. A year later I went on what I refer to as my happy drug, Oestrogen HRT. That was my solution. Yours might be completely different. The point is, you don't have to endure it. Our bodies are just doing what they're supposed to do, but that doesn't mean we can't treat them like an obnoxious child and do whatever it takes to put them in their place. We need to ask, research, and invest some time, effort, and if needs be, money that puts us somewhat back in control of our bodies. The key is to find the right doctor or specialist. Many GP's are not as knowledgeable as they should or could be about menopause. This has caused huge swathes of women to be prescribed anti-depressants for example, instead of hormone replacement. It is imperative you speak to someone who fully understands the symptoms of menopause and the variety of ways they can be addressed. If you're not confident about your own GP, find another, ask for recommendations or go to one of the growing number of menopause and women's health specialists

Menopause is actually just puberty in reverse. Then, all the hormones are rushing in like crowds on a Black Friday morning sale. Now, they are retreating, and not in an orderly fashion. I think about how I had a kit ready for my daughter and the 'little talks' and books I'd been giving her to make sure she was fully prepared and, if not exactly enthused, at least not embarrassed about the next stage of her natural development as she approached puberty. Did I do the same for myself? Of course not. I spent the first year having a hostile relationship with my belly, it being stubbornly against any attempt on my part to stop it swelling like a balloon, rolling its eyes at me in defiance like my teenager, tutting when I whizzed kale in the nutribullet, sneering when I shoved chocolate in my mouth. After years of me more or less controlling it, my belly now had a will of its own. Even my good friend who is a pilates instructor got one, although admittedly hers was like a travel-sized version compared to my industrial-sized one.

Every woman's experience of ageing and menopause is different. It's a slightly chaotic process of oestrogen and progesterone withdrawal and it will impact you in a unique way, because you are unique. Here's an important thing to know. Oestrogen is vital for your brain, heart and bone health. Now that we are living up to a third, or even half of our lives post-menopausal, we need to ensure our long-term health is maintained and the oestrogen deficiency is addressed. Women currently are three times more likely to suffer from Alzheimer's. Once women hit menopause, they take over from men for heart disease being their number one killer. And you've guessed it, women suffer far more from osteoporosis than men. While 80% of women experience symptoms of peri-menopause and therefore, hopefully, seek some sort of help, 20% don't which means they may not even think to address the long-term impact of hormone deficiency.

Whether you self-medicate with mindfulness, Merlot or shopping; seek support from friends, facebook or therapy; or need help from prescribed supplements, replacement hormones or change of diet, we are not our mothers and grandmothers. We can pick up books, join chat groups and seek support from a variety of places to get the information we need to minimise, eradicate or just understand what we are going through. There is no excuse not to take the time to invest in what is happening to you, through you, and within you.

> ***Research has shown that women who are informed and more accepting of the transition typically experience milder and shorter symptoms.***

The emotional stress of not understanding it, or hiding it from people around you, of not being able to talk about it, actually makes it physically harder. Human females now live a longer life after menopause than ever before which few other species do. We still very much have a function and role, and critically, a chance to devote some time to ourselves. Being a woman is a process, always a glorious work in progress and no part of that progress should be seen as lesser than another. So whatever your age – later thirties, early forties, late fifties; whatever your stage – ignorant bliss, WTF is happening to me?, peri, post or probably confused; get armed with information and then take action to ensure you are doing the best you can for yourself. See it as a natural part of your evolution and freedom from your perceived role as mother to others, to entering a stage where you can be a mother to yourself. And as for trying to age in an age of anti-ageing propaganda? I say fuck it to ageing gracefully. Let's age powerfully.

Audit # 2 – Your Body

This audit is about making sure you check out where you are right now from a health point of view, so you can put an action plan in place and function to your best potential. By body audit I mean an assessment of what do you need, what needs work, what aches, what are your fears, what are you tolerating but could really do without? What have you been meaning to do but never quite get round to – have you had a smear? Have you checked your breasts? Iron? Blood pressure? Please note this is not a once-off exercise. Investing in regular health audits should become a regular practice.

Let's start with what this isn't:

- An exercise in judgement

- ★ A hypochondriac's wet dream
- ★ A shame fest
- ★ Another thing to worry about
- ★ A comparison with perfection, whatever that happens to be this month, according to Instagram

Let's clarify what this is:

- ★ A check up
- ★ A check in
- ★ Gathering knowledge so you can take full control of your health
- ★ Getting an update on how your body is changing
- ★ Investing in yourself, your health, your ageing process so you can get on with being fabulous.

Depending on your age, your body will need different approaches to food, exercise, rest, wine, hydration, sleep, sex, moisturiser, brain function, and possibly even eyeliner.

Let's do two lists, one for the inside and one for the outside. How do you feel about each aspect? What is your family history? On a scale of 1–10 where do you feel each area is currently at? What one small action can you take to increase that number by 1? What information do you need to make an informed choice? Have you availed of free screenings?* Take stock. Then find a doctor who will support you properly through this time.

You can just journal this or look at or download a template on my website www.themidlifecoach.org/MidlifeRedefinedResources

Outside

- ★ Skin
- ★ Hair

- ★ Breasts
- ★ Belly
- ★ Knees
- ★ BMI

Inside

- ★ Brain
- ★ Heart – blood pressure, cholesterol
- ★ Gut
- ★ Libido
- ★ Screenings*

You might want to create another Wheel – this time of health, using the following headings:

- ★ Fitness/Movement
- ★ Eyesight
- ★ Nutrients/supplements
- ★ Diet – balance of foods
- ★ Family history
- ★ Sleep
- ★ Menstruation cycle/menopause
- ★ Hormone levels

**Free screenings – mammogram (from fifty), smear (every three years), bowel screening (from sixty), bone density (from sixty-five), Blood Glucose (from forty-five)*

3

HAVE I ACTUALLY *Just Ghosted Myself?*

★

WHAT AM I?

If my body was in free-fall, my mind was worried there was no parachute. Felled by grief and overwhelm, I tried to figure out how to navigate this new life, while also getting used to being old(er). That just felt too hard altogether, so I stumbled onto the easiest path, that crumpled road of least resistance. It's easier to shut down than to feel, isn't it? It's easier to shout, rather than try. During the day, I kept it together as much as I could for my girls, but as soon as they were tucked in bed, I raided the gin cupboard and switched on Netflix, losing myself in unrealistic TV drama, rather than face up to the reality of my own drama. Now separated, I had to create new ways for living, alone. But that felt too scary so I just did the alone bit. You know that cliched montage in the romcom movie of someone falling apart? The lounge is a mess, littered with empty wine bottles and pizza boxes, the sad soul has greasy hair, wearing stained sweat pants and possibly dribbling? (This was pre-covid, and so not the norm!) In the movie, that montage lasts about three minutes, or as long as it takes to belt out All By Myself. That was me. For a year.

I was also facing the most miserable form of torture ever invented;

single parenting.There is a reason why early humans only thrived in tribes, and it wasn't just to scare off hairy mammoths. Being left alone with a small feral child is not conducive to sanity. So menacing and demanding are babies and children, that you need a ration of at least six adults to every one child (To fact check, see the Encyclopaedia of Wall Carvings). I'd found it difficult enough when there were two adults to three kids. Now I was expected to do it alone, when I could barely fathom how to look after myself. How was I supposed to hold their pain, their confusion, their wants, needs and desires, when I didn't know how to hold my own? I'd lost my marriage, my mum, and seemingly my 'youth'. It felt careless, and the only way to wade through it all was to switch on autopilot, hoping I kept course, not even sure if there was a destination programmed in. Because women have perfected the performance of 'Fine', I still looked like I was functioning but really felt like a ghost; a translucent, faded version of myself. I was there, but not fully filled in, people seeing through me because my imposter syndrome wasn't a syndrome, but a reality. During marriage and parenting, I'd became disconnected from myself. On paper it had looked like I'd had everything – house, career, husband, kids, fabulous dinner parties. But in my heart I felt I had lost so much of myself, as if it had somehow been a trade: in order to have all that, I had to sacrifice me. I felt I'd been hijacked off the version I thought I'd be living. I felt ungrateful that I wanted more for the effort I was putting in. I was so busy performing like a circus animal, I forgot my natural behaviour. I was obviously shit at everything: shit at being a wife, shit at being a mother, shit at being a woman, shit at being. I was ghosting myself, not responding to my own calls, that voice from within that loves me but can't compete with the external pressures to be perfect. I was living life half-filled in.

Many of us fall into this trap, this unconscious way of existing: ticking boxes, making meals, manically moving but never going anywhere. We *re-act* instead of *pro-act*. We firefight instead of live intentionally. We switch on autopilot rather than look out the window and navigate in a deliberate manner.

All I did was do. On the surface I pretended I was coping, because God forbid one might show signs of actual dysfunction. That's not how we were brought up, thank you very much. We're told we can and should be super-women; having it all, doing it all, being it all, whilst simultaneously adhering to the latest dictates from the Fashion Fascists on how we should look, what we should wear and what we need to be ashamed of (last year it was big bums, now it is small bums, keep up, keep up!).

I looked after my girls, looked after my mum and when she died, supported my dad, returned as many painful marriage separation volleys that were fired at me, and worked, but I didn't partake consciously in any of them. I looked after everyone and everything, and forgot to look after me. I pretended I was ok, but inside was a tumbleweed of negativity and self-doubt. I was also really, really tired. I mean emotionally deranged, violently crushing, mad-woman-in-the-attic tired.

Burn, Baby, Burn

Burnout is a real and frightening experience and is increasingly common. A 2019 survey found that less than half of women (42%) said they were satisfied with their work, nearly 60% said they didn't get enough sleep, and nearly three quarters said they suffered from too much stress. This isn't the preserve of a few; overwhelm is becoming an epidemic. Throw in a global pandemic, where women took the brunt of homeschooling and family caring, *and* made up the majority of healthcare and essential workers facing unprecedented pressure both at work and at home, and many faced full-scale burnout.

Of course the best time to work out the answers to life's questions is 4.21am. Said no person ever. So why did my broiling brain think that was the best time to spring into action and start rolling in the mud-swamp of jobs to do (pressure), things I shouldn't have said (shame), conundrums like does micro needling actually work and can it make my cheeks plumper? (fake news), I should do more pilates (nagging, guilt, depression, inadequacy). I don't need to have a crystal ball to know you know what it feels like to be tired. Not that lovely 'just had a big walk in the country' tired when you want to sit by a fire and read your book. No, I mean that soul-crushing, weep-inducing, never-ending exhaustion that seems to have become an acceptable part of modern living. Between constantly juggling, worrying, comparing, delivering, meeting expectations and deadlines, we can end up in a cycle of perpetual tiredness.

You wake up every morning with a feeling of dread, patch yourself together for the day with a lip-liner drawn-on fake smile, dry shampoo, glow makeup that fails to make you look fresh just shiny, and 162 hits of coffee. Green tea just isn't going to hack it so you just invest in a litre bottle of Diet Coke; you never know, it might come with a slow-motion, bare-chested gardener who will momentarily take your mind off the fact you are so fucking tired you'd be pushed to come up with your mother's name if asked. Tiredness is like poison running through your body. Sleep affects every single aspect of your life – your mood, thoughts, energy, libido, metabolism, relationships, work. Yet apparently we aren't getting enough of it.

According to the UK's National Sleep Foundation, women need more sleep than men do to function properly. This is because the more you use your brain during the day, the more rest it needs at night. Women tend to multi-task, using more of their brain than men, therefore needing at least an extra twenty minutes of sleep. So let's not even think about our sleep deficit as a result of periods, pregnancies, night feeding, stress and menopause. Research shows that women can lose up to three hours a night as a result of their partner moving in bed (men tend to be bigger and therefore make more of an impact) and snoring. Generally women also sleep less because they are still on duty, even at night. This idea that once babies 'sleep through the night' you get your sleep back is a monstrous myth. Having had years of young children wake me, I now contend with teenagers keeping me up at night! So we are trying to survive busy days while sleep deprived most of the time. Lack of sleep can lead not only to mental health issues such as depression, but also physical conditions such as obesity, heart disease, diabetes and a shorter life expectancy.

I felt I had a permanent hangover, my head thick, my body sluggish and I found it hard to get motivated. Is it any wonder? Sleeping for only 4.5 hours has the same impact as having a blood alcohol level of 0.1%. At this level, speech will be slurred, and balance, vision, reaction times and hearing will be impaired. Motor coordination will be considerably impacted along with good judgment. It would be illegal to drive if this was alcohol. This means if you're not getting enough sleep, a drunk is in charge of your plane (which at worst is on course for a crash landing, or at best is on autopilot).

Conditioned to be nurturers, we feel guilty if we take time to relax. We compete with partners, colleagues and friends about how busy we are, as if it's a badge of honour instead of a slow suicide plan. Stress isn't caused by the umpteen jobs we think we have to accomplish, but by the pressure we put on ourselves to do them, and do them perfectly. It's living up to the Good Girl Grade, competing on a field where the opposite team are all airbrushed, starved, and fictional. You *have* to acknowledge that this is a tough and confusing time. Women aged between forty and fifty-nine have the highest rates of depression out of any age or gender. We are still not earning equal pay or pensions, and a 2018 UN report found that women still take on more than twice (2.6 times) the emotional labour in a home – and this is not just the physical housework but the mental responsibility for managing everyone. That's without even going into the #MeToo world of everyday sexism and sexual violence. I was listening to the radio one day and the female presenters were talking about our love for TV, 'flawed' characters like the Bridget Joneses, the Fleabags, the Emmas. I was about to nod in agreement, so conditioned am I, until I realised just how fucked up that was. They were celebrating these 'flawed' women because they don't have all their shit together. But doesn't that make them the normal women? Aren't flawed characters actually the unrealistic ones that are constantly shoved down our throats as being perfect? Who wakes up with an airbrushed face, a four-jogs/five-pilates-classes-a-week body, in a magazine-spread home, sailing through a meteoric career, with polite, obedient children, and a husband who loves your menopausal rages? No fucking one! We're not 'flawed' because we're crippled with mirror-hatred and are at risk of failing our juggling class. That's the norm!

Whether or not you have children or ageing parents, you are likely a carer in some form, carrying the care for all the other people in your lives.

> ***Being a carer competes with the rest of your life, and so it's imperative you make sure you are also a carer of yourself. Don't compete with other people, but compete with yourself to make sure you keep your life in the care plan.***

According to the Nagoski sisters in their 2019 book *Burnout: the secret to solving the stress cycle,* running yourself into the ground from the stresses of work, home and general life is one of the biggest issues facing women today. Being a woman often feels like a relentless stream of low- and high-level stressors that feel out of your control, yet are your responsibility. This is in large part due to the 'human giver syndrome' most of us suffer from – that feeling that we must always be attentive to the needs of others, and that we are selfish if we prioritise our own. We must be pretty, smart, capable, loving, giving, perfect, with great teeth, cheek bones (or at least good at contouring), keeping up with the Kardashian-dictated version of beautiful, lean in at the boardroom, and pick up dinner ingredients on the way home (because the Judgement Police are everywhere and processed food is punished by zero social media likes). For me, this pressure bled me of colour. On one hand I was trying to over-achieve, and on the other, I had given up, constantly sick, tired, and half-alive.

The power of pain

Midlife is also a time when we are likely to face some level of grief, be that the loss of a family member or friend, children leaving home or the demise of a marriage, relationship or career. Grief is the purest form of pain, and it changes you. It hurts so much you're sure you have internal bleeding. Conditioned to dislike discomfort, we often want to bypass the going through it, wanting a quick fix instead. But as I explored in my book *The Sandwich Years*, grief is like the Sunday driver in front of you on a narrow country road: you can't get past, no matter how hard you beep your horn and swear. You eventually just have to accept that this is the speed you are going at, and try to keep breathing. My mum had loved flowers, taking time to notice them wherever she was. Every February I would wait for her excited call to tell me she'd seen the first snowdrops, the sign that spring was on its way. I'd then get a series of follow-up calls as the crocuses, then the daffodils appeared to confirm that the dark days were over, the landscape filling with colour again. Around her first anniversary the snowdrops pushed up early, as if to wave at me: 'Hey there, start paying attention.' It was so painful to think of her, but as the landscape began to fill with purples, pinks, oranges and yellows, it felt like she was telling me to start colouring in my ghostly life again too. I thought back to that unfinished book, her life brutally cut off mid-flow, and it reminded me that everyone's life is a terminal condition. We will always be an unfinished project. We live in a world where we are told to be great at everything, achieve A+ or step out of the arena. But this isn't the Hunger Games. It's the Game of Life, and often we're using the wrong rules. The changes that impacted my mum's life meant she was left with no choices. I realised the changes in my life did not, no matter how difficult that may have felt.

What I have learnt is that to be alive is not about avoiding pain, but about making use of the inevitable pain that will happen. Pain hurts so much because it has power. Yet power has two potent opposing positions – it can destroy or it can propel. Which one you adopt is your choice. You can deflect it or accept it. Deflection is only temporary though; it will never go away, instead hovering like a storm cloud, an ever-present threat to your peace of mind. Accepting the pain, and then using its power to rebuild, means it will hurt. Hurt so fucking much you will scream into those lonely lost hours of sleeplessness. But in those screams something magic happens. Absorbing the pain brings the power within you, working for you, not against you. The power of that pain makes you stronger. The pain becomes your power. One of the most potent ways to use your power is to live for the aspects of your life you deem the most valuable. Not in monetary terms, but intrinsically. Everyone has core values that act as a sort of compass, and often when we feel life is off course and ghostly, it's because we aren't living aligned to those core values. Values are what you consciously and unconsciously believe matter most in life. We all have different values because we all have unique upbringings, cultural influences and experiences that impacted us. As children we learn a value system from our parents and school, and as we grow up we develop more from peers, cultural influences and our interpretation of experiences.

Along the way we can get side-tracked and buffeted by life or the expectations of others and may need to re-evaluate our values to identify what are the most important ones to us now. The values that drove you as a twenty-year-old might not serve you as well as a forty-year-old (eyebrow plucking, anyone?). Knowing your values simply helps you make decisions about how to live your life.

Tragedy taught me to wake up and get off autopilot, because the only way to make sense of loss and trauma is to build something good from it. I began to wonder what I would miss out on if my life abruptly halted the way hers had. There is so much I still wanted to do, experience, feel. I had so many dreams and ambitions, but they lay crumpled under the weight of the laundry basket. But I was suddenly more afraid of wasting time than I was of not being good enough. It wasn't just that I was half-way through my life; I was half living. I looked in the mirror, saw my ghostly self and knew I had to bring her back to life. I had to go back and figure out what was most important to me, what values drive me at my core, what forms my internal compass, what my life should be aligned with, not resisting. As I did this work, I began to see some clear frictions between the life of my values and how I was living.

My mum was gone but my values around family were not.

My marriage had ended, but my value of adventure and agency had not.

My body was changing, but my value of living life to the fullest, with zest and enthusiasm, was not.

Defining, and in some cases, redefining what my core values were, gave me the first point on my inner compass; the guiding lights that would give me some clarity as I stepped onto this incredible new landscape of midlife. Doing this work on values will help you write some of your signposts. One of my values is agency. Knowing this helps me make decisions around work and lifestyle choices, knowing how I want to feel, rather than what I think it should look like. I'm OK being self-employed because agency is more important to me than security, say (not that security isn't important, but it's not one of my core values). Someone with security as a core value will feel safer in a secure job. No value is right or wrong, but living a life aligned to your values will make it feel easier (note, I'm not saying easy, it will just feel easier).

Audit #3 – The Value of your Values

Values connect you to your intrinsic self, and help with decisions on how to move forward. Knowing your values can help you navigate difficult situations, and help you prioritise and declutter. They help you develop a strong sense of self, which increases your confidence and overall contentment.

1. In your journal, identify five situations where you have been happiest. Mix up headliners and small moments. Mine might include swimming with my girls in Donegal, publishing my first book, dancing alone in my kitchen, sitting around with friends shooting the breeze, and some travel adventures.

   Now for each one, identify four reasons that made it so happy. What are the common factors? Was it achievement, connection, creativity, helping someone? Write them all down and see what common themes emerge.

2. Now do the same exercise for five situations where you have been most proud (try not to make it about your pride in others, like a child. So if it's a child graduating for example, make sure it's because of the work you did to get them there. This is about you, and what makes you feel most ignited and inspired by yourself). Remember to identify what factors were at play that made you so proud: self-reliance, community, beating the odds, proving someone wrong?

From the above, can you identify your core values? There are some examples on my list of suggested values on my website www.themidlifecoach.org/MidlifeRedefinedResources but these are by no means definitive so if something else comes to mind, use it. List your core values and rate them according to how important they are to you right now (your values won't change but they may alter in priority over different times of your life). Then rate how much those values are being honoured right now. There is no judgement here – you're just trying to identify where there is a gap. Sit with how you feel. We'll be using them later, but for now, think how you can honour them more.

4

WHO THE *Hell Am I?*

★

WHO AM I?

Realising I had to colour myself in, I realised I was out of shape, out of touch with myself, and out of practice figuring out what I actually wanted. Discovering who we are can be a confusing thing for a woman. Partly because we are plugged into the patriarchal matrix from the moment we are born, shackled to the societal expectations of what a Good Girl should do and look like; and partly because we can get to a point when our sense of identity is more often than not defined by our relationship with others - daughter, sister, mother, wife, partner. It's not easy for us to declare who we really are, and what we really need. Instead we hide in plain sight, like Russian dolls, roles within roles within roles, often forgetting the solid nugget of us at our core.

> ***We spend so much time and energy trying to find people who get us, we forget to spend any time and energy trying to get ourselves.***

We are in constant conflict with how we feel and how we think we should feel, be and do. We're not sure about who we really are and so we pretend to be fine when we're not. We pretend we can manage when we can't. We pretend to smile, we pretend that our needs don't matter, we pretend that our to-do lists actually make us happy, using them as a stick to beat ourselves with. We pretend we are ok with the ideal of beauty being dictated by others.

Our external identity

Our sense of identity is often focused on the external body image. Historically, women have been valued for their looks and position in society as mothers, so when these change it's hard, until we realise we can step into this new space. Look how it's changing! Our mothers would never have seen women past the age of forty even present the news. But the great thing about midlife is we now have the war paint and battle scars to start shedding the shit that shrouded us. This is our chance to choose. Look how women of every age, at every stage, are rejecting that stale stereotype. But it's not easy. Like a lot of women, I've had a love/hate relationship with my body most of my life. Have I undressed and lathered myself in un-firming self-loathing as well as the firming lotion? Yes. I have a curvy figure and so because Kate Moss was the body ideal when I was in my formative teenage years, I came to 'believe' that my thighs, hips and boobs were something to be slightly ashamed of. Even at my marathon-running fittest, I was never going to be skinny, always curvy. Horrifyingly, I see how my teenage daughters are trying to squeeze their normal, beautiful bodies into a 'skinny' shaped mould, distraught and self-critical when surprisingly they can't. How many women have hated their body, linked their sense of identity to someone else's dictate of what the 'in' body type is? Our sense of identity is so linked to how we look, yet we have no control over the standards set of how we 'should' look.

In just the last hundred years, every imaginable body shape has been in style. From the busty, tiny-waisted Gilbert Girl, to the 1920s Flapper of no cleavage, no waist, or ankles on display for those Charleston moves. From the curvy Hollywood 1930s sirens to tall and angles (think torpedo bras) of the 1940s. Then the Barbie hourglass becomes the 'norm', and ads for bust cream appear in magazines. Suddenly Twiggy is the 'It girl' and an ad for girdles uses a picture of a pear, captioned 'This is no shape for a girl.' (I kid you not.) Then the long, lean Disco Queen, and it's all about legs and the onslaught of the Super Models. But no sooner have we stretched ourselves and bought the push-up bras than the 1990s Waif look becomes the aspirational body beautiful. We entered a new century but were bullied by the same old bullshit with the pressure of exposed, ripped abs and most women now just want to lie down and eat a bowl of Doritos. It's exhausting. None of this is real! Women come in all shapes and sizes, yet at any one time, huge swathes of them are made to feel unacceptable. I see women walk around shrouded in shame, because they will never be dressed in 'ideal.' Everything from our physical shape to our hair colour are held to account, bombarding our sense of self. The point is, beauty is a fully constructed thing. We are at war with our bodies instead of the beauty marketing bullshit. I see my daughters try on identities like discarded clothes in a changing room, various attempts littering the floor from someone's raised eyebrow or throwaway comment. What's in and what's not is decided by people who don't live in, yet dominate, our worlds. Our body shape is our body shape – we need to dress to impress it, not some Instagram trend that will be gone in a week and we'll be left with a cupboard full of bust cream/bum enhancers/diet pills, and deflated emotions.

There wasn't much I could do about my body shape except focus on getting healthy and I was happy to be tied to dyed hair. So in an attempt to identify myself, I turned to my clothes. But instead of seeing a wardrobe that reflected a woman in charge of her destiny, I saw a dressing-up box, outfits bought to fit the roles I thought I should be playing: the Boden bright mummy clothes, bold prints to cover up the fact I didn't have a clue what I was supposed to be doing; the crisp corporate outfits, not too bright, not too tight; the casuals that just resembled someone trying to fit in but not sure which gang they belonged to. There were so many versions of me I could have thrown a party and likely run out of glasses. I also had to try and find a Single and Dating Me look. I shut the doors and reached for the gin. My identity had grown cobwebs in the corner while I catered for the needs of family, husband, children, parents and job. I decided to throw out anything that didn't fit, look right or made me feel like an imposter. There wasn't much left. Now I try to dress according to my body shape and personality rather than forced fashion. Clothes should bring out, not hide, the 'you'. It doesn't matter how cool culottes are, they will always make me look like a bag of spuds, but a low-neck wrap dress will always work. Looking at the various personalities in my wardrobe I realised I had become what I chose to spend my energy on at the time; few of them were me. Growing up I remember my mum always asking me 'Do I look too young in this?' In her generation the worst crime you could commit was to be 'mutton dressed as lamb'. Now the worst crime is to look too old. So much has changed for women in just one generation we can feel adrift in a world that doesn't quite know what to do with us. This extra twenty years we've been gifted in the middle of our lives is unique but a bit like the 'teenagers' that emerged in the late fifties there isn't a clear definition of who and what we mid-agers are now. We are the rebels of mid-age, sometimes not sure of the cause. We have to identify with who we are. Not a forced body shape or style, but be confident, empowered and at ease with ourselves. Anything else is self-flagellation.

Who has seen 'night out!' scrawled in the calendar four days away, simultaneously eyeing it with both excitement and dread? Excitement because: Yay, I'm going out to engage with actual adults, take off my Big Pants, put on some decent underwear and hunt out the Charlotte Tillsbury lipstick, my gal pals, the fun, the craic, the 'Oh fuck it, let's have another bottle' kind of night. But then there's the dread because: I'm so fucking tired I hope we can get a seat, there's decent lighting so I can read the menu, and I can get home by 10pm so I can take off the tight-waisted jeans and get into my elasticated pyjamas. The evening arrives and we leap into the shower. In our minds we have dressed ourselves in *that* outfit. Yes, in our minds those jeans go with that top, our hair will behave, and we'll look slim and sexy and societally acceptable. But after the shower, remembering to exfoliate, shave our armpits and pluck various areas of our face and bodies, we dress, only to stare deflated and dejected in the mirror because we look nothing like we did in our heads. I mean, nothing. We bulge here, we overhang there and our underwear gouges our flesh so we look like we've got a back boob and three thighs. So we crumple deflated onto the bed before hauling ourselves up again to do the Wardrobe Ransack of Shame, the floor littered with the debris of defeat, and we either cancel or slump out in the Old Reliable Comfy dress wishing it was 10pm already and we were in our pyjamas. Why do we do this to ourselves? Who has done this to us? Who is driving the bulldozer through our confidence when it comes to what we look like? Models have no role if they're just a model whose body is their job and we're expected to match it. The role models are the real everyday women, short, tall, thin and curvy, squat, pear shaped, apple shaped, pineapple shaped, or whatever fruit is your passion shaped. At long last, we are starting to see some variety in advertising and fashion shows, but fuck, it's still really hard to just feel OK.

I gradually relieved myself of the labels and identities I had dressed myself in, and slowly began to choose a style, wardrobe and look that made me feel like me, not who I was supposed to be. Will I ever be accepted on Love Island? Not with these love handles, but the first step to identifying myself was accepting myself. My body got me places, it gets me places. I had three (yep ladies, three) C-sections so nothing, and I mean nothing is going to get rid of that little C-section shelf no matter how many Latin Dance video series I pay for on YouTube and then never do. I will exercise and eat healthily because I want to look and feel as good as I can, but I also want to find the balance to enjoy my life without the extra weight of body (image) snatching lunacy. I want to choose or not choose botox and be free from boxed in ideals.

Regardless of current fashion and ideals, my body is fabulous and here is why:

- ★ It's relatively fit. I couldn't run another marathon (at the moment, but always leave room for potential), but I can run a fun few miles with a pal and that's good enough.

- ★ It's relatively healthy. I put chocolate into it. I pour wine into it. I sometimes put crispy chicken dipped straight into the mayo jar into it. But I've made the decision that mostly eating healthy food is one of the ways I want to live my life, so I find the balance.

★ It's functioning.

★ It's not a perfect 10, but I wear a 12, and keep a little 2 for me.

★ It gets me from A to B, often via X, Y and Z because I'm a woman and we can never go anywhere directly without stopping at the post office, dropping off a child, picking up dinner, and buying some M&S beetroot sushi because your daughter has decided that's all she'll eat, and you love making her happy even though she hates you.

★ It carries my brain, which is like carrying several people some days (see below).

★ It likes warm hugs, and gives good hugs and there is nothing like the feeling of stretching in a downward dog or the warmth of a child in your arms (even if you have to do it when they're asleep).

★ It gives me pleasurable feelings in lots of ways ;-)

Learning to love your body – and doing so by finding the right balance of health and fitness – is one of the most important acts of rebellion you can do. You don't have to be 'perfect', just pleased enough to get on with enjoying life, ditching the dead weight of false shame and embarrassment. I don't want to be skinny but I want to be able to skinny dip without apologising for my wobbly bits. I could be 3kg lighter, but I enjoy chocolate and wine. I could be 3kg heavier but I like to keep fit and exercise. Balance isn't about standing on one toe to get the scales to behave, it's learning to be you, no apologies offered.

Our internal identity

If the external is a head-fuck, wait till you look at the internal! Who you believe you are, you will become. The power of your own belief system is critical to how you see yourself, yet often you believe stuff that was handed to you and never challenged. As such you can easily live an identity given to you by a distracted dad, an overwhelmed mum, jealous siblings, a catty friend, an abusive partner, a disenchanted teacher. You take a throwaway comment, a faulty narrative, a societal expectation and carve yourself out of other people's views. As you grow from child to adult you forge your personality to fit a script rather than from your own imagination, painting a picture of yourself using a colour palette that doesn't match the skin you are in. You spend so much time worrying about what others think yet rarely consider if they could be wrong. Those Russian dolls I mentioned? They exemplify perfectly how women layer themselves in roles until their core is hidden. The small solid nugget is you with all your innate traits and talents, quirks, likes and dislikes. But soon you add a layer as you strive to meet the expectations of your culture, society, parents and upbringing. You might then add a layer for your role in society and career. Then you add one as a partner, another as a parent, and finally, by midlife, you have formed the outer doll that contains all those layers. This is the one you present to the outside world composed of the Facebook happy shots, meeting the Good Girl expectations, the way things are done and all the ways you might conform and even contort yourself to fit in. It's not that all those layers are fake or necessarily bad. But they are roles you play, layer upon layer, often smothering the core inside. Reconnecting to yourself means turning on a light, the light you so often brightly shine on others, on yourself, on that core, looking at which beliefs serve that core and which do not. Looking at what you really want, and how you really want your life to feel.

The thing I discovered was that not only were many of the beliefs I had about myself not true, but that the ones that were revealed I was a confusion of complexity. I'd believed I was meant to be straightforward so I often hid or resisted parts of me that were conflicted.

> ***You are so conditioned to contort yourself into a neat little pigeon hole, pilates practice notwithstanding, you can fail to see that your uniqueness is your multi-faceted complexity.***

Being conflictingly complex is what makes you dynamic, not disastrous. There is no one else exactly like you, with your exact likes and dislikes, thoughts and feelings, talents and quirks, your unique

DNA and unique cultural blueprint formed from your specific family and school experiences. It's OK to be many things to many people, because the sooner you realise you are many things to yourself the more you can accept yourself in all your complexities. You are always striving to be loved for who you are, yet you might seek that through validation of what you do, and how you look.

We are where we spend our energy and thoughts. What dresses me most of all now, is my intentionality. But back then, as I stood in the confusion of a wardrobe that no longer dressed me, I realised that many of my beliefs about myself didn't either. If I was to colour myself in, I had to challenge the identity I had stepped into on autopilot and decide for myself which colour palette really suited who I am. When you accept your multiple parts, you get to challenge some of the beliefs you use as fact about yourself, instead of the fake news they might be; beliefs you aren't good enough, too much, too loud, too old, aren't pretty enough, smart enough. Beliefs that you can't do something or be someone because you haven't seen it or someone told you you couldn't. When your sense of identity is a script, handed to you by parents, schooling, friends, culture and society – when you're on autopilot – you don't ever ad lib or change the lines to ones that might suit your voice better. That's why, especially at a time of change, transition or stagnation, you must look at the script you are working off and decide what is the story about you that you want to tell. There will be parts of the script that are beautiful and enriching: values and strengths that you've taken from the legacy of your upbringing that still serve you very well. But there are other parts of the script that are out of date, or were written by someone in anger or distress that you have taken as the truth and then lived, when all along it was never true. It was just a parent perhaps having a bad day, a love-lost partner putting you down to make themselves feel better. To process your world, you place a narrative on your experiences.

> ***You don't see or observe things as they are, but through glasses tinted by the script you've been handed.***

You have to release yourself from the burden of feeling like you need to be something you can't be, or something you feel you'd like to be. These are called self-sabotaging beliefs, because they sabotage your sense of self and stop you feeling or being who and what you can (we'll deal with this in detail later on). You are born full of potential, a blank slate, but are slowly funnelled and shaped, conformed and confirmed until you have been moulded into a shape not always of your own making. You add yourself in as an afterthought but to live well, you have to start with 'Who am I?' and then every input and output feeds that. This is a challenge for those of you not used to self-reflection. I certainly spent a few decades, resigned until my late thirties, that my external and internal identities were two entities with only a small overlap. But in order to flourish, that overlap needs to be as large as it can be – your external connected and reflecting your internal.

We are taught to label ourselves, box ourselves in to one beautifully wrapped, perfectly polished package. The problem is that one day that wrapping could be a brown paper bag and the next a gold-embossed designer paper with matching ribbon. It's the expectation that we're always meant to be beautifully wrapped that breaks us. We hear a lot about self-esteem. But self-esteem is judgement of your worth based on external opinions. Self-compassion, on the other hand, is far more important, because it's based on embracing yourself. As you are.

This is your time: when the switch suddenly clicks that you don't need to give a damn about most of the external expectations; where you can wear your sexuality with confidence rather than pressure; when the apron strings that perhaps tied you to bad marriages and ungrateful kids loosen (maybe why so many divorces are initiated by women after fifty). We still have enough self doubt to always want to keep improving, but now we have time to explore that curiosity; about ourselves, our passions, our world, and most of all, our potential.

Audit #4 – Your accomplishments

I'm going to ask you to do something most women don't think they're very good at. And the ones that are tend to be called bossy and brazen, as if that's a bad thing. It wasn't the 'done thing' when we grew up, to shout about our successes, glorify our goal scoring, or brag about our best bits. Self-congratulation was not something a Good Girl did. If we are to redefine the way mid-age has been lived and perceived, abiding by the Good Girl rules of putting others first, not making a fuss, not being too opinionated, too proud, too anything is not going to support us. When someone compliments our outfit, instead of saying, 'Oh this old thing? Got it in the sale,' we could say, 'Oh thank you!' Instead of asking 'Does my bum look big in this?' we could say, 'I love the way this top makes my boobs look so good.' Imagine! Imagine if you pumped yourself up, rather than put yourself down? Imagine if you admitted you were good at stuff, rather than pretending you're not in case you offend anyone? Write down at least three (many more if you like) accomplishments/likes in each of the following categories. They can be as big as getting the job you wanted, running the women's mini-marathon or doing a course, or as small as surviving that family event without stabbing someone, coping with grief or just getting through the damn day you didn't think you would.

- ★ Career
- ★ Personal (just for you)
- ★ Relationships/friends/community
- ★ Spiritual/personal development
- ★ Health/fitness/sport
- ★ Body

How does it make you feel? Do you want more of those feelings? Keep going back and adding to this, and even put the list somewhere you can see it. Laminate it if that works. I have a client whose marriage ended unexpectedly just weeks after she was forced to retire. She was demoralised and needed to build herself up. As part of our work together, she began to build a list of every damn thing she has ever accomplished. She stuck it on her fridge and for weeks she would add something to it she remembered, or something new she had done. She said it made her smile every time she went into the kitchen. Who doesn't need that kind of empowerment?

5

HAVE I BEEN PLAYING BY *The Wrong Rules?*

★

WHY AM I?

One of the hardest challenges of being a woman, and in particular a woman approaching, or in mid-age, is the exhausting and often debilitating levels of confusion. I don't just mean the question of what sized bum is in this year, or is it no glasses, one glass or three bottles of wine that are good/bad for me?

A bit like emerging from a dark cave (where who and what we were allowed and supposed to be was strictly defined), we are slightly blinded by the light of this potential freedom, not quite sure which direction to take, possibly wondering if we need a permission slip to be signed for us. We have these extra decades of life to be lived, but no one has given us a handbook. For many women I coach, the hardest part for them is realising they have to sign their own permission slip.

Mid-age is essentially about growing up. No longer young, stupid and wrecked by insecurity; not yet old, wise and wrecked by arthritis; we are grown up, hopeful, and wrecked by the mayhem of life. We've followed all the signposts we were supposed to, but instead of arriving at a place of smug satisfaction (boxes ticked, thank you very much), we are more likely standing in the demanding glare of social media, slightly bewildered that the day always feels shorter than required, the effort seeming far more than the reward, and if only we could sleep, lose five kilos, drink less alcohol, drink more water, step up more, figure out how the bloody heating app works and look good, feel good, perform good all of the time, we'd be able to actually enjoy life.The ground is shifting under our feet, our landscape isn't what we planned, and our faces aren't photoshopped.

We're stuck in a rut. Restless. Short-changed. Trapped on that proverbial adult-sized hamster wheel because our heel is stuck in the spokes. Or we feel we want more. Or want less. Or want to slow down. Or get going. Or excited about our dreams and plans but not sure how to go about them, because the dinner needs to be made. Or all of these simultaneously while anxiously keeping up appearances on Instagram. We're also a little angry. Which is OK because on one hand, anger is the new calm: 'Fuck it' the new mindfulness mantra. On the other hand, we're told that anger doesn't look good on women, as if it were a gaudy plastic accessory to an outfit that doesn't quite match. Does my bum look big in this? No, but your angry face looks ugly; give us a smile instead, luv. We're happyish and like our 'stuff', but are frustrated we haven't 'arrived' at the promised destination, or we're there but the room overlooks the rubbish bins, the aircon control is broken, fixed at a chilly three degrees lower than is comfortable. We can't even raid the mini bar because every article we now read on Twitter tells us that women our age shouldn't drink any more. Surely this is EXACTLY the age we should be drinking? But no. Along with numerous gender gaps, patriarchal paranoia, a totally irrational societal narrative that any woman over the age of twenty-five needn't bother to apply for positions of relevance, a body that has gone on its own journey of transformation without telling us, we also have to deal with the unfairness of hellish hangovers. This is the time we deserve to down a bottle of Chablis after all the work we've put in, because why should youth get fresh skin AND hangover-free drinking? If age is giving us wisdom and experience, it should at least give us the liver function to enjoy it. It can all just feel a bit unfair (but we can't say that out loud because aren't we supposed to be so grateful for everything?).

It's also a confusing time in history to be a woman.Yes, we are redefining midlife, and yes, equality is finally being taken seriously and everywhere we look, women are breaking stale stereotypes. But then Trump happens. And #MeToo. Women are still being raped and murdered at a traumatic rate. As such, there still exists the deeply ingrained legacy of disempowerment that feels like an itch we can't scratch. When the film *Suffragette* came out in 2015, I remember feeling shocked, realising that just 100 years before I would not have been allowed to vote, because humans with wombs weren't accepted in the rooms of power. Somewhere in us still, we carry a bruise of doubt that we're not yet considered good enough; that 'women's' issues aren't 'real' issues. When a man writes a novel about a man on a journey of self-discovery it's called a masterpiece. When a woman writes about a woman's journey it's called chick lit.

There is a lovely scene in the last season of *Game of Thrones* when Arya, who has spent her life (literally) fighting the Good Girl box everyone wants to put her in, turns to her sister and says, 'I knew what I was doing was against the rules. But he [her father] was smiling, so I knew it wasn't wrong. The rules were wrong. I was doing what I was meant to be doing, and he knew it.'

The rules are wrong.

> ***We're confused because we never wrote the rules and we know that many of them are wrong.***

Amid all this confusion, it's no wonder our minds feel like a riot, with 6,000 thoughts a day jostling and elbowing, grasping for attention, pushing and pulling our mind until we just want to tell ourselves to shut up, especially at 4am. Isn't it ironic that women have been given all this extra time, yet none of us feel we have any time? The more life we've been given to live, the more busy we become to distract us from living authentically and intentionally. With competitive to-do lists, we mistake 'doing' with being. What

I've learned is that if I'm too busy being busy, I'm busy not being.

> ***You hear so much about renewable energy, but your time isn't, yet you are constantly giving it away for free.***

If you are so preoccupied with getting 'there', you may get to the end of the road without ever looking up and realising that 'there' is here. When is now. How much of your life have you been awake for, rather than on autopilot for some distant destination that you think will make you happy when you arrive? Social psychologist Daniel Gilbert's research discovered that people are notoriously bad at predicting what will make them happy, yet those expectations shape our thoughts and decisions. He likens us to incompetent gamblers hoping to hit the happiness jackpot, but ending up disappointed, in debt and confused because we did everything we were supposed to. Like the pressure of New Year's Eve where if we expect it to be fabulous, it rarely lives up to the hype, we have expectations of lives we'd like to live, but are too busy living the life we're in to get there. Don't, do, have, ditch, gain, lose, reach, stretch, reduce, lean in, lean back, step up, step down, tune in, tune out, turn on, turn off, eat this, stop eating that. Is it any wonder we're confused and switch off because our brains hurt?

> ***Crippling expectations create a dissonance between what we think should be and what is, and takes away the joy of the moment, and the future.***

Expectations take away all the possibilities of what could be and what is, by highlighting what is never guaranteed, or somehow even realistic.

How do we unwind from the triple bind?

Women are confused because of a triple whammy of expectations that Dr Stephen Hinshaw and Rachel Kranz describe in their book *The Triple Bind: Saving our teenage girls from today's pressures and conflicting expectations.* The first is the pressure to be good at all the traditionally female stuff: be nurturing, kind, understanding; place others' needs above our own; throw themed birthday parties; maintain an immaculate, on-trend home freezer packed with nourishing meals;

dress with a vague nod to this century's fashion trends; work out every day and meditate. We're expected to be wonderful wives, marvellous mothers and fabulous friends, while also caring for our ageing parents, dancing like nobody's watching and making our homes plastic-free. The second pressure is to do all of that while also now being good at the traditionally male stuff, smashing the glass ceiling in non-laddered tights. Having mastered (mistressed?) the first expectation, we have pressure to get great grades, amazing jobs, kick ass (and balls) in sport, and run the household budget on a colour-coded spreadsheet. This means being strong (physically, emotionally and mentally) so we can lead, manage, mentor, control, assert and direct, which places us on a confusing challenge to also be nurturing, kind and co-operative. When women are expected to fulfil contradictory roles at the same time, it places us in constant turmoil. No matter what we excel at, we're failing at something else. In the early nineties Dr. Mary Pipher called this the double bind, revealing how it was devastating to the mental health of women and girls. Twenty years later, Hinshaw and Kranz realised that not only had things not improved, but that there is now a third bind. This is the expectation that our value is somehow linked to how well we conform to an ever-narrowing standard of thin, hot, and sexy (while making it look effortless).

Something has to give, and for once it doesn't have to be you.

Going into recovery

The turning point for me was a trip to Spain which had been booked prior to my marriage ending. Thinking it would be the best option for the children, my ex and I decided to split the holiday because we were stupid and sore. (Note to anyone who is in the stupid and sore stage of a breakup: please ask a person who has come out the other side before you make any stupid and sore decisions.) I took the girls out for the first half of the week, and their dad was to take over the second half. Even as I write that I can see how stupid and sore that idea was. But in that period of open wounds and warfare, it seemed like a really adult, mature decision. I was a gibbering wreck, disguised as a functioning woman. Obviously, with hindsight he should have gone first, but instead I arrived at 11pm with three small children aged four, seven and eight, searching around in the dark for a suburban villa with a grumpy taxi driver I couldn't communicate with, and then, having eventually found it, tried to get the girls ready for bed while figuring out the light switches and aircon. It was the family villa of my ex-husband's work colleague, and was dark, cluttered and 'lived in', and my girls were frightened. Despite plenty of bedrooms, they all slept with me that night, and every night of my four days. The next day was spent trying to figure out where we were (miles from shops and beach), buy food (on a Sunday), and generally get to grips with the fact that none of us actually wanted to be there, while I wore my forced happy face, determined to make it FUN (jazz hands). However, I was beginning to understand the particular hell that is single-parent holidaying where every single parenting thing is down to you. Of course by the time their dad arrived, I had stocked the fridge, figured out the landscape (dutifully drawing out a map) and got them settled so that all he had to do was waltz in, take over and play. I will never forget the pain of walking away from my children, even though he was the one who had walked away from the marriage. I stood outside the villa gate listening to their squeals of delight dancing with the splashes of their pool games, wondering how I was going to carry both my suitcase and heart which had now burst free from my chest, to the taxi. I had decided to stay on for a few days in a nearby AirB&B. Alone over the next couple of days, the fear and frustration I'd kept bundled tightly up inside so I could pretend to be a functioning person burst out of me like air from a pierced balloon and I eventually collapsed in a fevered heap. I became so sick an excruciating abscess developed in my armpit, my body literally poisoned by the swamp of grief and horror I was drowning in. I managed to get on a plane to Belfast to stay with my dad, and in my state of utter collapse, tried to manifest him waiting for me at Arrivals. He wasn't there. Adjusting my voice to Coping Mode, I called to tell him I'd arrived, just in case he was actually in the car and on his way. He wasn't. He wasn't, of course, because having been brought up never to be a burden to anyone, I'd told him not to bother picking me up. Sobbing in the taxi, I finally stood dishevelled and weeping at his front door, shaking and close to passing out from the infection in my body. He was shocked when he saw me. He was shocked because I'd never allowed him to see how badly I was doing. He was shocked because I hadn't been able to articulate that I'd needed him to collect me from the airport and look after me please, thank you very much. That night, with antiseptic wipes, he drained the abscess until an egg-cup full of pus had flowed out of my armpit. Next morning he took me to his GP who repeated the procedure, then fixed it up and gave me antibiotics. She also put her hand very decidedly on my leg, stared directly into my eyes, and told me to look after myself.

I nodded, not knowing what that meant. I did the caring. I didn't know how to ask for it for myself. I was sufficiently shocked, however, that my body had been so poisoned by my emotions – thoughts and feelings that had focused not on me and my recovery, but on the betrayal and the pain – to know that something had to change. Buddha knew what he was talking about when he said, 'No one saves us but ourselves. No one can and no one may.'

I'd felt I was being skinned by a potato peeler, strips of skin removed bit by bit, but I realised that the wounds weren't healing because I picked at the scabs and watched the glinting metal of the peeler rather than nourish my skin and focus my energy on the new potential as it grew back. As long as a dead marriage, missing mother, and midlife confusion was where I spent all my emotional and physical energy, dead, missing and confused is what I would continue to be. I slowly began to divert my thoughts and energies to myself and immediately my health improved.

> ***Who you are is often a reflection of what you spend your thoughts on.***

Where you spend your thoughts, who you hang out with, what you think and talk about, is who you are. What you watch, who you follow, who you listen to, who and what you read, is who you are. Where you invest your energy is what you become.

I had to stop putting my focus on the potato peeler and start focusing on the new skin I was growing. I did two things. The first was realising I could ask for help. Over the next few years I sought both personal and professional help from friends, family, counsellors, advisors, experts (and I was so transformed by this I went back to college to train to help others). I also took the brave step and went into recovery.

Not for the gin, but for the perfectionism that was ruining my life, draining it of colour. After years of feeling I was gasping for breath, I grabbed my own oxygen mask and started breathing again. It's a commitment I have to keep making because I don't want to be good at being someone else, or someone's version of who I should be. I want to excel at being me.

I'd always believed that putting others first and pretending I was coping was what I was meant to do. But that wasn't what was best for me. It's not what is best for you. And that is one of the most confusing dilemmas women face. It's hard to focus your energy and attention on yourself when you have been conditioned not to, but that egg-cup full of pus, and making that decision about where I would focus my thoughts and energy, would change the trajectory of my life. It will change yours. You have been given an opportunity no generation of women have had.

That is your fucking permission slip.

The most radical self-love I have learned was to allow myself to be vulnerable, ask for help when I needed it, stop putting my external perfection before my internal needs, and to start mattering in my own midlife. No one else is going to sign your permission slip. Not because they don't love you. But because they have their own stuff going on, they may not like change and most importantly, no one else is responsible for your happiness. Just as you are not responsible for anyone else's.

The more you understand the overwhelming, contradictory, and ridiculous expectations being placed on you, the more able you will be to redefine yourself in ways where you define the rules. After every coaching session I ask my clients what has been their most important take-away this time. I love when sometimes they look up and say something along the lines of (and these are the actual words of one of my clients): 'My life needs to be more about me.'

Saying 'yes' to you doesn't mean blowing up your life, but using your elbows to make room in your life for you.

You're a work in progress. Perfectly flawed, and you have the right to flourish as you. Imagine how your life might be different if you really believed this: I have inside me, at all times, my whole potential.

Accept yourself for who you are – perfectly flawed. Understand you didn't write the rules and turn confusion into curiosity, fear into fuck it, and give yourself a break, because let me tell you, no one else will.

Audit #5 – Your strengths

This is the final audit before you switch off autopilot and take control of the aircraft. You've done audits on your life balance, body, values, accomplishments, and now you finish with strengths. Knowing your strengths helps you work to your best side, knowing that you can rely on them when you need them.

When I was younger I was often told I was too much, too loud, just 'too'. Yet as I travelled and built my life and career, I knew that that 'too-ness' was often what pushed me, so I was confused. As part of my training to be a coach, I did my first strengths audit. Zest came up as my number one strength, and it immediately made sense to me. Now I know it's the thing that can push me through and bring so much magic to my life. I also know there are times I need to harness it because it can be overwhelming both to me and to others. My zest can lead me to burn out, as well as create my magic, and so learning how to manage it to my advantage has changed everything. Now I know I'm not 'too' anything, and that if I harness my zest and energy in the right way I am unstoppable.

Knowing what you have in your armoury makes you so much stronger in the battle. Knowing your strengths will help you know who you are, and give you the confidence and self-assurance in yourself no in-season lipgloss can. The key is to then make sure you turn those strengths – the things that make you such an amazing person to others – on yourself. I had a client whose top strengths were fairness, loyalty and kindness. But when we looked, we could see little evidence that she was using them on herself. So I encouraged her to ask regularly, 'Am I being fair to myself? Am I being loyal to myself? Am I being kind to myself?' Seeing yourself as the most important relationship you have will change your life.

You can either do a survey among loved ones and colleagues to gather an idea of your strengths or you can do a free online survey. VIA (Values in Action) was established in the wave of positive psychology a decade ago, and twenty-four character strengths were identified across all people and ages, divided into six classes of virtues.

- ★ **Wisdom and knowledge** – creativity, curiosity, judgement, love of learning, perspective
- ★ **Courage** – bravery, perseverance, honesty, zest
- ★ **Humanity** – love, kindness, social intelligence
- ★ **Justice** – teamwork, fairness, leadership
- ★ **Temperance** – forgiveness, humility, prudence, self-regulation
- ★ **Transcendence** – appreciation of beauty and excellence, gratitude, hope, humour, spirituality.

These character strengths are the qualities that come most naturally to you. We all possess them to some greater or lesser degree, giving each of us our own unique character profile. When you know your strengths, you can use them to improve your life and thrive. Research shows that people who know and consistently use their strengths are eighteen times more likely to flourish than those who don't. This survey takes about ten minutes and is free. Look at your top five strengths and really journal about how you use them on yourself. Look at the bottom five and ask how you can nurture them more.

Ready? Go to www.VIAcharacter.org

SECTION TWO:
Midlife Design

★

COLOURED MARKER AT *The Ready!*

★

Pus-free, and in perfectionist recovery, I now needed to figure out how to open my parachute to stop the freefall of autopilot I was hurtling through with no destination in mind. Just because I'd realised I needed to take charge of my life, didn't mean it all fell into place, setting off immediately with my compass, map and a backpack full of emergency chocolate. I'd felt choice-less for so long it took a while to realise I could make choices again. Longer still to learn how to do that.

The first step was to stop believing the narrative that I'd no control of my life. That in itself began to set me free. Psychologist Dr Edith Eger in her powerful book *The Choice* explores how the power of choice is the only real power we have. Victims, she explains, ask 'Why me?' Survivors ask 'What next?' It's not about what happens to you, it's about how you respond.

Over the course of the next year, step by tiny step, I unfurled my parachute by deciding how I wanted my life to feel. Then I began to live a more intentional life. As the MidLife Coach I realise how many women are still grasping around in the G-force, jowls flapping, desperately grasping for the release cable too. This section is about taking a firm grasp of that parachute cable, giving your flapping jowls a break and steering so that you guide your parachute wherever it needs to go. It's about constantly asking yourself not what do you need to do, but also, simply, what do you need.

Change is happening whether you like it or not (change has been happening all your life, it just perhaps feels more turbulent now). The key is whether you fly through this time on autopilot, or in the pilot seat: by default, or by design?

Here's the good news (gratitude, and all that). If you feel you want more from life, an ember of hope cradled in your gut, that isn't in fact, indigestion. The good news is that for the first time women can do just that – breath oxygen into that ember, feed the flames and get more from life. Look back to see all that you've achieved between twenty and forty, and now realise that's only half the amount of time from forty to eighty (which we now know is the most ground-breaking eighty in history). There is a landscape littered with sign-posts of possibility and potential that haven't been pre-written yet. You can change anything, and that knowledge changes everything. Every habit, every routine, every belief, every goal, every reaction to a trigger … you can choose to change them if you believe they are not serving you.

> ***Every action you take is a choice. You either make it passively (on autopilot) or actively (intentionally, by design).***

You have so much potential, but often you're surviving day to day, rather than thriving in glorious splendour. You're also scared. Frightened that perhaps if you really looked at the things that bring you joy, boost your energy, or spark an ember of fire in your belly, it might upset the carefully constructed life you have cultivated. It might upset other people. It might make people think you are a bit uppity: 'Who's yer one over there with the notions?'

> ***Autopilot means your life might be a response to a fear of upsetting people, or a constant search for validation from expectations that aren't even about you.***
>
> ***Living with intent means your life is a reflection of who you are.***

The fear is valid. I see it every time I catch a glint in a client's eye when she allows herself to think about carving out space for real joy in her life, before a shadow subdues that glint: the shadow of shame, guilt and the conditioning that we are supposed to nurture, care and capitulate; not choose, design and proactively put ourselves in the driving seat of our lives, putting ourselves first. The thing to remember is that when you are happier, your loved ones will be too. Frustration happens when you fall into a default mode you never chose. Rather than plan the next step, you ruminate on the last one. Rather than focus on possibilities, you assume you can't do it differently. Rather than taking charge of your life, you feel powerless. This book is not called *Eat Pray Love*. No one is expecting you to run off to far flung lands (unless you actually want to).

It will involve you figuring out what you want. It's a shift because you've been conditioned to meet demands, deadlines and standards, so you're cautious about venturing out into the open space of intention, without the crutch of the needs of others to hobble along on. That's normal.

For too long, women have been so caught up in the blizzard of busyness, they have forgotten how to put themselves on the to-do list. This is your time to make a choice to proactively live your life consciously, intentionally, passionately, fiercely. To live a better, bolder, brighter midlife. It is the decision to find your authentic potential rather than your virtual potential. Because there are two versions of you. There is the Authentic Potential that floods from the core of you in those Russian dolls: who you really are and who you really want to be, and what you really want your life to feel like.

Then there is your Virtual Potential: the outer doll working off a prescribed script which we all adopt and adapt to. The pre-written signposts I talked about; other people's version of what success looks like; what you think you're supposed to be doing, feeling and achieving; how you're supposed to look by Instagram standards; how happy your family life should be as per Facebook eyes; how busy you're supposed to be in order to get validation; how beautiful without being fake, how excellent without looking like you've tried. Your Virtual Potential can be exhausting because it's not real! It's a fictional construct dictated by society, social media, Good Girl expectations and a patriarchy that serves neither men or women.

There may be nothing too wrong with this Virtual Potential – it's just that it's not specifically formed by and for you, with your personality traits, quirks, talents, skills, strengths, your desires and dreams. It is usually a one-size-fits-all off the rack rather than something bespoke to the skin you actually live in.

So designing a valiant and vibrant midlife – redefining what your midlife can look and feel like in this unique and unprecedented opportunity – is about trying to live your authentic potential rather that your virtual potential.

By the time you reach midlife, you're a patchwork quilt. You might have started off with a clear vision of how you wanted life to be, then you added extensions, styles on top of styles, papering cracks, until you look like a house on the outside, painted front door and trimmed bushes, but inside you're a higgledy-piggeldy collection of good rooms and non-functioning spaces with no natural light, and clutter. Now you get to be an interior designer. It's uncomfortable because default mode may feel easier. Yet default is actually really uncomfortable, but because you know this particular brand of discomfort, you stick with it. To live your life by your own design, you have to make the choice to move into the unknown discomfort of growth.

You are at midlife, at a crossroads. You get to choose, *really create*, perhaps for the first time in your life, how you want to carry on living. Turn left and you carry on on autopilot; turn right and you start driving this baby. Your choice. When I talk about designing your life I don't mean in the artistic sense (although that's often a part of ourselves we squash down to accommodate the washing pile and work demands). I mean it in the sense of CREATING: creating the optimum thoughts to make something happen, creating space, creating time, creating habits, creating opportunities, creating goals, creating plans to achieve those goals, creating a life of intention. The core of creating? Choice.

That's all it takes: proactively, actively choosing to invest in yourself; money (maybe), time, energy, love, thought, permission. So expect this section of the book to feel like Pilates for the Brain. It will involve stretching, resistance training, flexing, building repetitions and using muscles you may not have used before.

You've done the audits – you've taken a helicopter look at your life, your body, the times you succeeded, your values and your strengths … now let's use them to design the life you love.

6

WHAT DO *I Want?*

★

BLANK PAGE

Woman walks into a shop. Wants 'something nice' to wear. Three hours later, after fifteen try ons, a changing room cluttered with discarded clothes, tears, tantrums and a snorting of chocolate, she stands sweating and slightly defeated in the queue, holding clothes she doesn't really want, but because she definitely wants to come home with *something,* these will do. She'll either return them, keep and never wear them, or wear them and feel like shit. Sound familiar? We can have all the choice in the world but unless we know what to choose, it's just more mayhem and confusion. Walk into a shop with a clear idea of what you want – a knee-length blue dress, say – and your eyes will seek it out, dismissing everything else. No need to run your hands over rails of clothes wondering will they make your bum look big.

We've never been taught to ask for what we want. If we ever knew. Instead, we might ask what do we want for our family, work, relationship, but for us? Not so much. That's why I started with discovery, going back to look at your strengths, values, definition of achievements so you can start living in the right direction. Deciding what you want is the beginning of the design phase – not based on external demands, but on internal needs; not what everyone needs from you, but what you need for yourself.

What do you want?

Whether you call it manifesting, designing or deciding, it is simply the act of creating in thought, a life you want, based on a desired outcome. An architect needs to know if it's a three-bedroom house or a one-bed studio before she starts designing. A fashion designer has to know if the clothes she is creating are for winter or summer. The known outcome is necessary before the design can begin. That's why in the Wheel of Life I asked you to think about what a higher score would look and feel like for each section. What would make the difference? Imagining and designing is the first step to becoming. I don't mean dreaming of winning the lottery and then waiting optimistically for it to happen. Especially as in my case, I do this without actually buying a ticket. That's clearly delusional and doesn't recognise the actual work you have to do. It also doesn't mean some woo woo wand waving, expecting a big house and the Diet Coke guy to appear in a puff of magic to mow your lawn without doing anything to make that happen yourself (more's the pity).

> ***To make your midlife meaningful, you have to take the time to really think about what you want: see it, clarify it, make it tangible in your mind so that you can make clear decisions and choices about how you want your life to feel and look. Then live your decisions by taking actions to make them happen.***

By thinking about something you want, you immediately create its possibility. It might mean going off-script but by creating the possibility, you change everything. Here's why. Your brain is wired to seek confirmation bias, which simply means you look around to find confirmation of what you believe. You look around for friends, Twitter and other social media, you read and watch news that more or less matches your view of the world.

> ***So it goes that if you believe you can, you will be far more attuned to seeing, hearing, reading, believing anything that confirms that. Exactly the same as if you believe you can't.***

You may think you have little control, but when you understand you can control your thoughts and direct your energy, you can create any life you want. If you actively design what you want your work/life balance to look and feel like, you will see the opportunities that will make it happen. Simply put, what you are thinking, you attract. The minute you are trying to become pregnant, all you see is pregnancy. If you believe you are too old, your brain will select and highlight everything that confirms that. The exact same information and events are available or happening, but depending on where your thoughts and energy are directed, your brain will unconsciously select and highlight the information and events that confirm what you want or think. *So where you direct your thoughts and energy is key.* You focus on the potato peeler, you'll feel only pain. You focus on the potential, you'll feel the inspiration. Life is simply energy, and what you focus your energy on is where you will be. Living a life by design not default means creating the life you want to live in your mind, and then acting intentionally to create it.

Psychologists have long used the concept of visualisation as a way to help people attain goals, change emotional states, and boost performance. Sports people will use it as a matter of course, because research has proved that you can improve your ability by visualising the perfect shot. Tennis and golf professionals are trained to see themselves hitting the perfect shot over and over again until their brain sees it as a reality. Seeing something in your head improves your ability in real life. When I was training for the Dublin marathon, the coach made us run every part of the course over different runs in the weeks beforehand. She made us visualise running that route and crossing the finish line. When the going got tough – and it got really tough – my brain already knew I had run it, and so there was no 'I can't' in my head, only 'this is hell, why did I do this, I can't wait to lie on the ground and never get up, but I'll keep going until then.' The latter is far easier to handle mentally than the former.

Your greatest liberation is deciding how things can be. You actually do it quite naturally without realising it, except often you are doing it negatively, by repeatedly telling yourself you can't, or should, or don't and you believe that version as truth.

Your definition of success

One of the easiest ways you can design your life is to think about your own definition of success. Often we adopt our definition from others – others who may well not share our particular strengths, values or desires. It's so easy to be swept away by the off-the-rack one-size-(doesn't)-fit-all success scenarios, never checking to see if they suit us in all our unique complexities. We put away our own desires and dreams when we think we have to please everyone. We quieten our voice because it sounds selfish, and it becomes quieter and quieter until we stop listening to it at all. Or like in my case, it comes out in shouting and anger. What I have learned, is that the louder my internal voice has become, the less loud my external voice needs to be. (Unless I run out of cups because they're all still in my kids' bedrooms gathering mould. That's just a shouty scenario and I've accepted that flaw in myself!)

Your adopted idea of success, or virtual potential, might not have been formed of your own design, but from an idea of success derived for a world designed for men. Or from your parents' expectations or an airbrushed Instagram post. Your life has moved at a pace, and what was a reasonable definition of success in your twenties might not feel so right now that you've experienced some of those ambitions. Your opportunities have changed too. What was possible for women twenty years ago is different now. For me, what does a successful post-marriage relationship look like? (I like to joke that I want to take a man's shirt off, not iron it, but I'm not really joking.) Relationships can be whatever way you need and want them to be. You are no longer reliant on the prescribed formula. What does a successful life feel like when kids have grown up now that there is freedom to travel, work remotely, be financially independent? These are the questions you now get to ask: who were you before you were taught to be and do the way you are? If you had a blank page, what would you write, draw, doodle? And I don't mean you create a life that doesn't exclude the reality of your current life – parents, kids, partners, career. But what next? What if? What would need to change?

I recently went to a talk by Irish business woman Andrea Horan. After her father died she quit her successful marketing career to travel. On that soul-searching trip she decided not to return to her old career, but instead use her talents to create a business that would allow her to live a life she actually wanted to live, rather than the corporate treadmill. She and her sister designed a nail bar in Dublin, so far removed from the traditional clinical model, it was based on the beach she was sitting on – loud, fun, full of colour. Tropical Popical became an instant success, enhanced by her marketing prowess (you even get offered a can of Lilt when you arrive).But suddenly it became a global success when Irish actress Saoirse Ronan was getting her nails done there when her Oscar nomination came through. She texted her excitement from the nail bar. She then mentioned where she'd been when she heard the nominations on the Ellen Show. Suddenly Andrea was inundated with advice and offers to expand Tropical Popical, not just nationally but in New York and LA. But because she had already defined what success looked like – and felt like – for her life, she knew that other people's ideas of success were not hers. Hers was to create a business that would give her enough time and income to travel, plus give her a platform to springboard her other passions – art and activism. If she had followed the traditional (perhaps male) idea of success, she explained, she'd certainly be 'successful' in business terms, but would most likely be so overwhelmed running a multinational business she would no longer have the time to live the way she wanted. She had defined what success looked and felt like to her, and then built her life around that vision, not being sidetracked by others' ideas of success.

Defining what success means to you means your life is lived on your terms, not someone else's. You are far less likely to get derailed by unexpected circumstances. Without knowing how you want your days to look and feel, they can be full of uncertainty and derailment. You are evolutionarily wired to replace uncertainty with the worst case scenario, and so intentionally deciding or designing is a way of creating a positive space in which you get to choose how to respond to a situation, directing your energy based on your vision of a successful life. Without manifesting your intention for the day, it is hijacked by external forces – the news, work deadlines, other people's moods, the weather and you can drift along with no skin in the game.

As I began to think about my definition of success for my life, I developed a clear picture of adventure, not drama (and I had often confused the two). A life lived creatively and courageously. But also one where I was on the to-do list, a life where time for me and my nourishment is built in to my lifestyle, not as an optional extra. That meant battling the belief that being busy to the point of overwhelm was the only way to be 'successful'. Now, because I know what success feels like, I can make choices accordingly and am far less likely to be drawn into a way of living that I haven't thought out. It meant turning my energy away from pain and the past, and directing it on me and my future.

In principle this was a great idea; in practice, I realised it was a long time since I'd really asked myself what I wanted, other than short-term comfort snacks. But at least I'd started asking the right questions: how do I want to spend my time, where could I be directing my energy, what kind of person do I want to be? You know, the easy ones. Sometimes it's easier to start with what we don't want. I didn't want to feel everything was an uphill battle. I didn't want to waste my life worrying about what had already happened or what might never happen. Over the course of the next few years I tried many things, and kept some. I decided to date again. I switched off Netflix, and started going to bed earlier, reading, opening up my brain to possibilities and ideas. I made a mad decision to go to Buenos Aires to learn tango. I decided to go back to college. I took up windsurfing, tennis and eating healthy foods (some of the time). My relationships with everyone improved, especially my children. But the relationship that improved the most was the one with myself.

Name your game

When I had started out as a nervous, lacking-in-confidence writer with babies at my feet, sending out articles and pitching ideas to editors, posting blog posts every week from a corner in the playroom, and slowly building the beginnings of a book written in snatched moments from my domestic duties, I was advised by a great writer friend that I had to start calling myself a writer. I had to become a writer in my mind to became a writer in reality. This doesn't mean I didn't have to not get up at 6am to write, or attend writing workshops to sharpen my skill – the work still had to be done. But deciding that this is what I was significantly helped my confidence, credibility and capability. Because I saw myself as, and called myself a writer, I showed up every week to my blog, even if I was sitting on a mini toddler's chair. Because I saw myself as, and called myself, a writer, I showed up every week to class and awkwardly read out my words. Because I saw myself as, and called myself, a writer, I sent ideas to editors and then followed through on the ones that were accepted. That blog? Written in the early morning hours about the pain and joy of caring for my mum, the pain and joy of caring for small children, the pain and joy of finding out the hard way what happens when I fail to care for myself, words written not knowing who would read them but needing to write them anyway because I was a writer? That blog caught the attention of a publisher and led to a book deal for what would become my bestselling memoir, *The Sandwich Years: a book about love, loss and dirty dishes.* None of that would have happened if I hadn't allowed the possibility to exist that I was a writer, by seeing it, creating it as a real and tangible label, before I was ever published. Pressing send on every blog post didn't make me a writer. Seeing my name in magazines and newspapers didn't make me a writer. Getting a publishing deal didn't make me a writer. Creating the positive space in my mind that allowed me to make the plans and sacrifices it took to face a blank page, plough through drafts and edits, and build my craft made me a writer. I became a writer regardless of if I'd ever been published.

You create the life you want to lead with every thought, every response, every action, every dream and every choice. If you see what you want, if you direct your energy towards it, if you manifest how you want your life to look and feel, that is where your habits and beliefs will take you. It's in the doing that the real magic of manifestation exists. Rather than drifting in a fog formed by external events, influences, triggers, and others' definitions of success, you simply give your brain a vision to focus on, a signpost to follow ahead. Every single moment of every single day you are making choices, whether you're aware of it or not. (And more often than not on autopilot, you're not aware at all.) From the moment you wake up you choose (or default) how you embrace the day – with clear intention, or with your head stuck in Facebook. Intention doesn't mean a long to-do list either. Intention can mean deciding that whatever happens, you are going to choose peace over chaos, adventure over drama, connection with real people over connecting with the internet, prioritising a conversation/task/balance over being run ragged by overwhelm. Manifesting what you want from your midlife means you know what you want. And then it's all down to your beliefs ... which is what we deal with in the next chapter

Decision #1 – Your definition of success

One way to do this is to ask the Miracle Question. (This is not about waking up and the miracle is you've won the lottery!) I want you to pretend you've woken up and a miracle has happened. You wake up and feel life is how you want it to feel.

What is different? How does it feel? What does it look like? Who are you? Write it out, draw it out, journal it out, think it out, talk it out. What does it feel like in your body? Now think about what got you there. Go back and look at your accomplishments, values and strengths. What else is true now? Engage your senses. Bask in it. What about in five years? Ten? We're going to get more specific as we go on, but for now, start defining what success looks like now and in the years to come (remember you have no control over anyone else's thoughts or behaviours, just your own). The more you feel it, and the more you practise, the more you start to show up.

7

TO BELIEVE OR NOT *To Believe*

★

OBSTACLES

How did you start your day today? Did you roll out of bed and before you even took a decent breath did the day's demands, expectations and the needs of others grab you by the throat and not let go? Or did you take a beat to think about what you need and how you want to feel today? When you become intentional about choosing where to direct your attention, you'll be less driven by your emotions. Realising you are not at the mercy of your emotions will affect almost every aspect of your life. Many of us think our feelings are the reality, but they are caused by all kinds of factors, with one, some or none of them being the actual truth.

In order to make a life-saving reaction to a serious threat, our brain created a fast-track process that bypasses the rational thought response to a trigger (like a rustle in the long grass, that might or might not be a dangerous snake) and go straight to survival reactions such as flight, fight or freeze. Today, on the whole, we don't find many snakes in the grass (just on Tinder). But our brains treat everything from work emails, social media comments, money issues, feelings about our thighs in relation to the girl on Instagram as rustles in the long grass and so 'to survive' we leap straight to the nuclear option of stress, panic, worry, and anxiety. It doesn't have to be that way though.

> ***You can't control everything that happens to you in life. But you do have the choice about what to think and believe.***

The key is to be aware enough, and intentional enough, to create that beat between trigger and reaction. To have a clear target to direct your energy and thoughts so that you are less likely to be pulled off course, or at least if you are, you can course correct quickly. If you can create a beat to avoid bypassing the rational thought, you can develop a response that serves you the best.

It's easy to get into the mental space where you think that life happens to you, external to you and you just react to what is happening. However, everything that really matters happens inside you. You can't control the rain but that's not what will impact you: it's how you think about the rain that matters – is it something you can just get an umbrella for, or will it ruin your day?

> ***Your attitude to anything, changes everything***

There are always other ways of looking at things. I heard a story about an alcoholic father with two sons. One follows in his father's footsteps, struggling through life as a drunk, while the other becomes a successful, sober businessman. However, when each are asked, 'Why are you the way you are?' they both give the same answer: 'Because my father was an alcoholic.' The same circumstance, the same childhood, two different outcomes.

Imagine there is a line in your mind. Above the line you are present, conscious, choosing how to respond, driven by your values and vision of success, focused on the big picture, open, creative, solutions-focused. Below the line you are distracted, on autopilot, reacting according to deep-seated patterns and behaviours, pulled by external drama and others' expectations, prisoner to the small picture, clenched, problem-focused. We can spend huge swathes of time below the line. So start asking yourself regularly, where am I? In this moment, am I above or below the line? It can mean the difference between a snarky, quick-fired angry reaction and a more thoughtful, long-term considered, understanding response. Below the line is a place of patterns we may have created as children to deal with a home situation but that no longer serves us as adults. It is a quagmire of thought loops and bored beliefs that go unchallenged. It is a cesspit where fear, defensiveness and shame thrive.

It's so easy to live a fiction born of our fears and other people's opinions. It's a lie but it becomes our reality. It could even have come from how your (much younger, unwiser) self interpreted an event. The event is the same, but your interpretation of its meaning and impact are *your* reality and perhaps different from someone else who was there. The story you tell yourself is just that: a story. A version. Rewriting a particular story doesn't mean you make stuff up. It means you look at it from another angle. I had a client who had a very traumatic experience in relation to her eyes. It knocked her confidence and derailed her completely. At one point, I asked her – from a safe distance now of being better – how else she could write the story she had on repeat. She came back to me the following week amazed. She had forgotten all the lovely things people had done for her, and how much support she'd had. She had been so caught up in a story of her eye trauma, she had been blinded to a wider picture. She reframed the experience and saw it as a resilience building exercise, and a realisation she can overcome serious situations. She has less fear because she knows she can survive being vulnerable because she has a net of people who will support her.

You can challenge the narrative you have created and create one that serves you better. Then be intentional and hold yourself accountable for every thought, action and response.

> ***What happens to you is an objective reality, how you respond is a subjective choice.***

You can't be responsible for everything that happens to you, but you have total responsibility for the way you interpret and respond to it. I don't want a middle-aged belly, and yes it's caused by a redistribution of hormones and reduction in metabolism, but given that, how can I take responsibility for not letting that be an excuse not to exercise and eat better? Dating in the twenty-first century is akin to the ancient gladiator games. Ok, given that, how can I take responsibility to make sure I waste as little time as possible by setting clear boundaries?

Below the line, the word 'should' reigns supreme. Above the line, you make active choices based on your intentions. Don't ever be lured into that murky place of thinking if everything isn't perfect, something is wrong. Life is never perfect, but you get to chose the problems you are prepared to live with. As a single mum, I chose the problems and flexibility of juggling freelance work and home life when my kids get back from school, over the problem of having to be in an office between set hours and finding child-care. It doesn't make working from home easy, but I chose one set of problems over another. Rather than be ruled by actions you 'should' be taking, make choices to do things that will align with the feeling of the life you want.

There are four things that make us different from other animals (apart from the use of toilet roll). They are self-awareness, imagination, conscience and free will. Yet often we just ignore them because we are so far below the line we are drowning in damaging thoughts and beliefs. We think our thoughts are real and we have no choice over them. Every now and then, pause and ask, 'What attitude am I bringing to this experience? Is it going to push me into a negative space, or a positive space? Am I coming at this from below or above the line?' Once you start to observe your thoughts as a slightly detached entity, you'll see how irrational they can be at times. You'll see your petty teenage self. You'll hear your hurt twenty-something self. I can now stand back and observe my thoughts fighting with each other over whether I should eat the chocolate in the fridge, like I watch my girls fight over who does the dishes, with an air of bemused boredom. Once you detach your identity from the thought, any thought is possible.

> ***Once you see and feel the power of that beat, you can insert it more and more between the trigger and your reaction to get a response that serves you better.***

How many times do you carry around huge boulders in your handbag of stuff that has happened, is never going to happen and that happened ten years ago? Buddhists call this the second dart. The first dart that hits you is the event. This could be a comment, an email, a rejection, a teenager not putting their cup in the dishwasher. Yet more damage comes in the form of the second dart – the one you fire at yourself, the feelings of abandonment, injustice, slight, hurt, anger, indignation. The pain from the second dart – all created by your thoughts and feelings – causes far more hurt than the first. Especially when I lose my reason over the abandoned cup and Armageddon ensues. (I really must deal with the cup issue.) We fill the noise with endless thoughts about what should be, how we've been wronged, how we are failures, instead of accepting the situation quickly and stepping back into a place where we are back in control, above the line. Our shame gremlins take up all the space and we end up causing a lot of our own pain. It's the underlying and overwhelming expectations that keep us stuck, overwhelmed, and feeling bad about ourselves. There is nothing wrong with wanting to be a good mother, partner, friend and colleague. The expectation of what it takes to BE all of those things has multiplied exponentially, so that no matter how much we give to these roles, we feel like it's never enough. How many times have you let your day be ruined by some stranger in a car who can't indicate or cuts you up? You spend the next fifteen minutes ranting at someone who is long gone, calling them an arsehole and then heaping on rants about all the arseholes you've ever known. This is me when I'm below the line. When I can catch myself above the line however, I like to play a little game. It's called What's the Best Case Scenario? What is the best story for this guy cutting me up? Maybe his wife has gone into labour and he's rushing to get home. I don't know the story. He may just be an arsehole or his partner might be in labour. It doesn't matter. What matters is which thought will serve me better so I can stay focused on my intentions rather than be dragged away by external distractions.

Gratitude is an attitude

So for survival, we are evolutionarily wired to fear the worst. Which means to thrive, rather than just survive, you have to actively reach for the best. You have to proactively turn your attention to the positive, amid the quagmire of negative. Cultivating an attitude of gratitude isn't just an airy fairy platitude to hyper positivity. It is a life-enhancing choice to direct your energy and thoughts in the direction that serves you best. From focusing on the best of you rather than the 'worst', pushed on by your strengths rather than pulled back by your 'weaknesses', buoyed up by your achievements rather than dragged down by your 'failures', to recognising and acknowledging the everyday moments that make you happy and contented. Understanding and practising gratitude has been one of the most important changes to my life that I am, well, grateful for. Gratitude doesn't make all your problems go away, it just makes them less shouty and in your face, because they are countered by more of the good things in your life. It's also important to note that gratitude is not another stick to beat yourself with. It can't be done on the basis of 'I should be' grateful for X because somebody else has Y. It has to be a genuine feeling of relief, recognition, joy, thankfulness that this thing/time/place/person/weather/ passion/ thought/skill/learning/moment/connection/chocolate bar is in your life at this exact moment. Like turning your face up to the sun and realising that it doesn't just provide light to the world, but warmth on your face, and in that moment you feel more alive. Gratitude is also not a mask to hide real feelings of pain and hurt. Feel the feelings and then be grateful for something amidst that pain. Gratitude has to be felt, not thought. It has to be real enough to boost you, because attitude is a choice, not a reaction.

To believe, or not to believe, that is the question

Most of my life I told myself I wasn't a runner. This was despite the fact that for most of my life, I have donned trainers and moved in a fast fashion. Growing up, both my dad and brother were runners. Like, *real* runners. My dad ran marathons and my brother was a long-distance runner who became an ultra-marathon runner. And so somewhere along the way as a teenager, I developed a belief that only people who ran marathons were 'runners.' Over the next few decades I regularly went running and even ran a few 10km mini-marathons. Yet, because of my belief that only people who ran marathons were runners, I never called myself one. I even would often say this to my running buddy Carol, while running! We sometimes aspired to being those people who ran marathons but I would always say, 'I'd love to, but I'm not a runner. My limit is 10km.' I said this with such conviction it never once occurred to me to question it. Then for my forty-third birthday Carol bought us both registration for the Dublin marathon. I'd have preferred a Mac lipstick, but I didn't want to seem ungrateful so I smiled and agreed to join a training group with her. Even as I began the training, I didn't believe I would actually run the marathon and so mostly went along to keep her company. I assumed I would bail once I hit my 10km limit. Yet something miraculous happened. Slowly building up our distance, one weekend we got to the 12km run. The previous one had been 9km. The miracle? Despite reaching, and then exceeding, my 'it's-such-a-fact-it-must-be-in-a-manual 10km' limit, the world didn't implode. Neither did my legs or lungs. The 10km limit that I had believed in for three full decades of my life was a figment of my imagination. It was a totally fabricated belief that I had never once questioned. With one step over an imaginary line, I realised I had taken fiction for fact and created a belief so strong it had limited my ambition, my potential and my thoughts. I realised the only thing stopping me was not my body, but my mind. I'm not going to tell you I eventually glided over the marathon finish line with my perfectly made-up unsweaty face. I hobbled over the finish line looking like something akin to a White Walker, but I ran that fucking marathon and the prize was not the medal. The prize was realising I had told myself – and believed – something that wasn't true about myself. The prize was challenging my beliefs to places I couldn't have imagined. I began to challenge other things I'd told myself without ever questioning it.

Self-limiting belief: I'm not sporty (because I didn't like hockey at school).

Self-empowering belief: I actually am very active.

Self-limiting belief: I'm selfish (because my mum called me that when I was a teenager and I didn't realise EVERY mother thinks their teenager is selfish, because biologically, THEY ARE!).

Self-empowering belief: I'm actually really kind and generous.

Self-limiting belief: I'm can't sea swim (because I'm not one of those people who likes cold).

Self-empowering belief: I can push through the initial discomfort of cold and discover I am a frickin' mermaid.

Our self-limiting beliefs often show up in the following ways:

I can't.

I shouldn't.

I should.

I'm not.

I can't lose weight.

I shouldn't take time for myself.

I should say yes.

I should say no.

I'm not good enough.

What you tell yourself about yourself matters more than anything anyone else will tell you.

Breaking those belief barriers set in motion a personal quest to challenge as many of my beliefs as I can, not to break them all, but to make sure the ones I have are based in fact, and aren't actually a figment of my unreliable imagination. Because that's how we have to treat our beliefs, like an unreliable narrator of a book. As a reader you perhaps know the narrator has an agenda, or doesn't have all the facts, and you can see they are making decisions based around that flaw – the version of events, the narrative they have constructed. Once I realised my beliefs could be challenged to see which ones were unreliable at best, and damaging or limiting at worst, so much more has become possible.

Identifying the belief is the first step. Just catch yourself saying 'I can't', 'I should', 'I'm not'. Then you have to seek its source by simply asking where it came from. Did you form the belief from an interpretation of an experience or event? Did someone in authority tell it to you, like a teacher or parent? Did you absorb it from a cultural perspective? Then question the reliability of the source. Could your interpretation have been blinded by immaturity or emotional distress? Was the teacher or parent just having a bad day? Was the cultural perspective wrong? Women used to be told they couldn't own a home in their own name, or hold certain jobs lest their hysterical tendencies broke the controls. Those rules, those cultural perspectives, were wrong, yet people believed them. Sometimes just seeking the source is enough to start creating cracks in the belief. Once I realised I had formed the belief that only people who ran marathons were runners as a young teenager, intimidated by the performances of my dad and brother, I immediately realised how ludicrous it was.

Next you have to ask, what is the proof that this belief is right? Did I actually have a 10km limit? There was absolutely no proof of this (because I had never challenged it!), and unless I was a medical mystery, millions of others have in fact proved that humans can run more than 10km. So I realised the source was ludicrous and there was no proof. Yet I had held that belief for thirty years.

When I work with clients, we look at beliefs that are holding them back. We seek the source of that belief, and then we look for proof. Almost without fail, if it is a self-limiting belief, the proof shatters it into pieces. You can't lose weight? Really? Never? You can't find love?

Really? Never? You can't make a speech? Really? You've never spoken to a few people? It doesn't mean suddenly everything is easy. It means though, that you change 'can't' to 'I possibly can' and sometimes that is enough.

I worked with Katia who is a busy mum, living in Ireland but originally from Russia. I heard her say several times 'I'm no good in social situations' as we looked at ways she could build up time for herself and build a community around her. So I challenged her on this iron-clad belief that she was no good in social situations, a belief that was holding her back from joining clubs and groups. (Especially since she had joined one of my group programmes and had spoken well and contributed throughout!) I asked her to find the source of this belief. She thought back to her childhood where, as a young girl, she was told to stay in the background and be quiet. She absorbed a belief that no one would value what she had to say. Then I asked her for proof. Yes, there were situations where she had felt extremely uncomfortable in a crowded room. I pointed out that she had joined a group workshop I had held, where she had to speak in a group. She said she was good at one to one, and could also manage small groups. I pointed out that that then made the phrase 'I'm no good in social situations' already redundant. She thought about more and more times she had actually been OK in social situations. We were able to reduce that blanket belief – I'm no good in social situations – to a much smaller spectrum of – I can get uncomfortable in large crowds. Already the power of the limiting belief is drastically reduced. It is now something you can work with. It is one of my favourite things to catch my client's self-limiting beliefs and watch them realise they can change it.

The next step with any of these beliefs, once you've sought its source and looked for proof, is to find a more supporting belief. The simple power of persuasion starts with the type of words you use in your thoughts and speech to yourself. I didn't leap from 'my limit is 10km' to 'I can run a marathon tomorrow' because there's a lot of training between 10km and 46km. The most important words you ever hear are the ones you say to yourself. My beliefs became about my potential, not my limits. 'I'm going to try and see how far I can get.'

With Katia we worked on changing her belief 'I'm no good in social situations' to 'I get on OK with people in certain situations' and 'In some social situations I can feel a bit shy, but not all.' Then I got her to take it a step further to create nurturing beliefs. 'I am working on being more calm in social situations.' 'I know I am really good when I am one to one and so will focus on that rather than the big crowd who aren't watching me anyway.' There is a world of difference between 'I can't' and 'I'll try' or 'I might.' Converting your self-limiting beliefs to supporting beliefs can be done in a number of ways.

You can make a giant leap. If seeking the source and looking for proof are enough to shatter the belief in one go, you can leap simply from 'I can't' to 'I can.'

Or you may need a middle step by creating a bridge to get you from a long-held belief to a new way of thinking. This is simply a shift in mindset (and then action) from powerless where there is no change (*I can't/I don't /I should)* to empowered with the possibility of change (*I will try/I will be open to/I am thinking about/I could /I might/might not).*

Or you can take a gradual approach. Many self-limiting beliefs are grand sweeping statements that allow no room whatsoever for nuance or experimentation.Taking out the defiance and adding in gradual growth allows you to get comfortable at each stage. So over a period of time, incremental steps will make a shift.

'I don't like healthy food' to 'I'm going to try and be more open to trying new foods and hope to build up a few healthier options when I go out' to 'I'm being more open about trying healthier foods and there's a few things that have surprised me. I'm slowly realising lots of foods I've labelled as 'healthy' are actually just food and they're quite nice' to 'I'm eating more healthy food than I used to' to 'I'm proactively choosing a more balanced diet. I still like my treats but I'm balancing with a range of new foods that I also like but which are good for me.'

I can't say this enough (not a self-limiting belief, because I've challenged it and it's true!) – **how you think is how you will live.**

Challenging your thoughts and beliefs is a process but one that will liberate you from so many invisible chains tying you down. It's important to remember that shifting self-limiting beliefs is not about just saying positive mantras. The shift has to be felt, believed and actioned. A helpful reminder is that proactive beliefs tend to be in the present tense.

I am doing

I am trying

I am going to

I have talents

I have a commitment to

You have the power to create your own torment, but you also have the option of choosing peace. Choose peace. Choose 'I am not my thoughts or emotions'.

It's not what you look at that matters; it's what you see.

Decision #2 – Identifying your self-sabotaging beliefs

What do you believe about yourself, others and life that limits or sabotages your happiness? What do you tell yourself regularly that begins with 'I can't' or 'I don't' or 'That's not who I am' or 'I'm not the kind of person who …'

Write down the belief. Now look for the source. Really explore this. Then look for absolute proof that the belief is true. Absolute proof. The slightest chink opens up possibility. Now write an alternative, empowering belief, either by leaping, creating a bridge or plotting a gradual pathway. And then never, ever stop.

8

AM I HAVING *A Growth Spurt?*

★

IDEAS AND DREAMS

Why does growing up imply we can't keep growing? One of the worst disservices we do to ourselves as we grow up is thinking that as soon as we're old enough to buy a G&T in a bar, and pay for it with money we've earned ourselves, that somehow we have finished growing. We focus on growing old, instead of just growing. We're so busy leaping valiantly into life, eagerly following the pre-ordained signposts without looking left or right, acquiring and accumulating status and stuff, we forget we ourselves are ever-evolving beings. Harvard psychologist and author of *Stumbling on Happiness* Daniel Gilbert notes that 'human beings are works in progress that mistakenly think they're finished.'

After the first couple of years being separated, I slowly began to see the time my kids were with their dad as not just a loss to me, or a time to catch up on sleep. I turned my energy on the potential gain, rather than the loss, changing my mindset to see that this wasn't just time I needed to kill, but time I could use to live. Vibrantly, for me. Having started to design a life where I could find the fun and adventurous side of myself again, I discovered a resort in Greece that gave me the framework to participate in yoga, Pilates, cycling, and some fun evenings but also enough freedom to do my own thing if I needed. Embracing my decision to push my comfort zone and try stuff I've always believed I'm not good at or wouldn't like, I went on the (uphill!) bike rides, I did strange yoga-esque contortions, and I tried to windsurf. It was weirdly exhilarating, so I kept trying, pushing away the thoughts and beliefs that I couldn't become a 'windsurfer' because I was a mid-aged woman with cellulite thighs and a penchant for Doritos. Because I'd learned from my marathon that what I believe will end up true. I returned each year, to connect with my body and mind through yoga, bike ride up hills I thought I would hate, and windsurf. Am I any good? Of course not. And that's the key with learning something new at midlife. We're used to being good at things, our hobbies and habits, our careers and comfort zones having all been perfected. We're used to being accomplished and so the fear of being a beginner can stop us starting new things. The first three attempts at windsurfing, I spent most of the time coughing up sea water. I couldn't read the wind or remember how to turn, but I kept going. Then it happened. I caught the wind without thinking. I was zigzagging the bay and riding the waves, baby! Of course in my exuberance I forgot how to turn and ended up half way to Kefalonia, only saved by the rescue boat who tottered up to me (naturally filled with twenty-year-olds). 'Fancy coming back to shore?' asked a rather handsome young boy-man. I smiled, nodding, 'Oh you know, loving the wind. Man.'

He smiled, tootling alongside me. 'Have you forgotten how to turn?'

I smiled back. 'Yes. Completely.'

I didn't care. They got me headed back to shore, and I was riding that sea, reading that wind and even though as soon as I got near a boat I lost my nerve and fell in, I still didn't care. The exhilaration of trying outweighed the frustration of failing. Every time I go back to Greece, I'm a little better. I still fall in lots, I still forget which way to turn, I still need the odd rescue. And I DON'T CARE.

Because growth isn't about being good. It's about feeling good.

Growing into your authentic potential

Your emotional development should last a lifetime, and midlife is a stage when often, after years of living on autopilot, you can re-emerge, slightly dazzled, into the light to peel back the identities you have taken on like the Russian dolls, challenging limiting beliefs, re-discovering yourself again, and deciding what's next in these extra twenty years you've been given. Rather than growing outward, collecting stuff and status like shoes, you can grow inward, exploring the wondrous expanse of you, shedding self-limiting beliefs and tuning in to your core and inner voice.

Your memories are half-truths. Your thoughts are, at best, guesses. Your expectations or predictions of the future are a gamble. Yet you can clutch them to your chest like a life buoy: set stories, set rules, set expectations that will keep you exactly where you are. Learning that your stories, past, present and future, can be interpreted differently means you are not bound by bias and handcuffed by history. It means you can grow in ways you might not have imagined. Constantly growing is essential to figure out your authentic potential – not the one that might have been prescribed to you, but one that really matches who you are. Your life story isn't set in stone. The story you tell yourself at fifteen, or eighteen, or twenty-three of the life you think you want to live, might not be the same story you would write at forty, or fifty, or sixty, knowing what you know now, and having experienced what you've experienced. Yet often you stay with the old script. Growth is about being open enough to let your story evolve with possibility. It's about making sure you're always the central character of your life, not the people, responsibilities or prescribed expectations handed to you by 'society' and an outdated culture. If your story is based on this kind of house, this is where I live, this partner, this job, this weight – and then something happens to upend that – they become the central characters of your life, not you. If you hang your happiness on something that is out of your control – how someone else thinks or behaves, an expectation not of your design, how someone else values you – you will never be happy. Growth allows you to keep them as the subplots and twists, while you move through the main story with curiosity and courage. You won't like all the twists but they can still have incredible meaning for your character development. Growth means not surrendering all your potential authentic joy for an idea you used to have about yourself that might not be true any more, or may never have been true. It's OK to rewrite your story from time to time. In fact, it's vital. Your authentic potential is who you can be *because* of all your traits and talents, your personality strengths and values, your courage and ambition, your sense of what will bring you peace of mind, and what really fits and tingles the skin you live in, *and* despite what happens to you. What you believe about yourself becomes your destiny, so make sure your beliefs are steering you in the right direction.

> *If you change the way you look at things, the things you look at change.*

At some point in your life you've probably come across that sketch, where a first glance reveals an old crone, but if you shift your brain slightly, the drawing suddenly transforms into a beautiful young woman. You are like that drawing: what you see dictates your interpretation of who you are. Women are grey. Not just grey-rooted but grey, as in not black or white. We are complex, complicated creatures. So when you explore who you really are, understanding you are a glorious work in progress, a woman who can grow and change and try new things, you can be liberated from those fixed ideas and ideals, to explore and grow ideas and ideals that will let you evolve.

Growth mindset

My twin nephews Tom and Alex were born premature at thirty-one weeks, weighing in at just over 1lb each. They were in incubators for weeks, and then when home, had to be fed through tubes and eventually by bottle every three hours. It took an hour and a half to feed, change, and put them to sleep, every three hours, so the maths isn't good for having any kind of life. When I asked my brother what advice he would give to other parents of twins for an article I was writing for a parenting magazine, he said the only way to survive was to manage your expectations. He gave the example of how, exhausted and in desperate need of downtime he and my sister-in-law Charlotte would plan a takeaway to be delivered at 9pm on the Friday night. They hung all their hopes on sitting down at 9pm Friday night, babies fed, burped, changed and rocked to sleep for the fourteenth time that day, balancing plates of chicken tikka masala and lamb biryani on their knees, the naan bread loitering between them, nothing to be heard but their sighs of relief and the scrape of forks on china. The success of the whole day, the whole week, hung on that expectation. Naturally 9pm would come and go, cartons of rice and curry stiffening in a warm oven, the house reverberating with angry screams of frustration, the twins also crying, until each over-tired parent individually scoffed spoonfuls of food straight from the oven, while the other over-tired parent soothed an over-tired baby. Placing that expectation on the success of the day made everything far worse. Growth is about learning to change expectations that don't work for you, or freeing yourself altogether by stepping into the expanse of what will be. I can almost feel my old self have a panic attack come on as I write those words. That old me needed to control the outcome of everything (because, hint: I felt in control of nothing) which is why she was continually spiralling in a tailspin. My current self now (mostly) prefers to glide, which can feel harder but the view is so much better.

Growth is moving through every moment as freely as you can, not limited by expectation. Psychologist and researcher Dr Carol Dweck has spent decades researching the differences between what she calls Fixed and Growth mindsets. In her bestselling book *Mindset*, she explains these two distinct approaches. With a fixed mindset you think your intelligence, skills and talents are static; that you are who you are, and can't (there's that word again!) change. Everything is about the outcome, and if you fail, it's all been a waste. With a growth mindset, however, you believe you can develop your intelligence, skills, talents and learning and adapt to change. It allows you to value what you're doing regardless of the outcome.

So believing they can't change, someone with a fixed mindset who has a desire to come across as smart may have a tendency to avoid any challenges that will threaten that, get defensive or give up easily when obstacles come their way. They resent and ignore useful negative feedback, feeling threatened by the success of others. Someone with a growth mindset embraces challenges, strives to overcome setbacks, sees effort as a way of improving, asks for and learns from feedback, finding lessons and inspiration from others. We all know the person who doesn't get the job and blames the interviewer. Then there's the person who quietly emails the panel to thank them for their time, and asks for feedback so they can improve themselves for the next interview. It's possible to have a fixed mindset about one thing (for me for a long time, this was not being sporty), while having a growth mindset about another (attending writing workshops and courses to improve my skills). We naturally teach our children to have a growth mindset, yet don't necessarily keep it up as adults. My youngest daughter Ruby was learning joint-up writing, and, frustrated she couldn't get it right immediately, threw down her pen. 'I'll never be able to write properly!' (I know you're now shouting 'that's a self-limiting belief'!). As an adult, I know all it takes is practice, so I helped her with the hard letters, explaining that I'd found it hard too. Nobody does it perfectly first time. Like her sister Daisy learning piano, you have to learn and practise and put up with not being as good as you'd like for, sometimes, a long time. My middle child Poppy likes to bake. If it works she thinks she's a perfect baker, but if the next time she tries something and it doesn't go well, she decides she's no longer a baker, and again, I have to tell her that baking is a life-long learning curve, that after thirty years of it, I still have catastrophic soggy bottoms occasionally. It doesn't make me a good or bad baker, just someone who needs to pay more attention next time, or google how to firm up my bottom (on oh so many levels). If you get fixed on certain ideas, ideals and expectations about the way you or your life 'should' be, you lock yourself in a cage. But if you open up your thoughts, challenge your self-limiting beliefs, stretch out your imagination through growth, you will unlock yourself, expand your horizons, and in doing so, recognise you are capable of far more than you thought.

Growth is about looking outside your comfort zone, occasionally taking tentative steps over the boundary, being prepared to experience discomfort to broaden that comfort zone, making it bigger, more creative, more connected, more satisfying, more resilient to change, and you become stronger, wiser, more experienced, more trusting of yourself. The thing about comfort zones is that they don't remain static. They are more like a muscle that needs to be kept flexed and used, or else it will shrink. The only way to keep your comfort zone from shrinking is to grow it. You can see this with some older people who appear to lose confidence. Or women who have been something to someone for so long, they've lost the confidence to be themselves again. You might think your comfort zone is a safe space, but in fact, it is an ever-shrinking cage. You've probably heard the phrase 'stepping out' of your comfort zone, but really it's about pushing out the boundaries of your comfort zone and making your safe space bigger.

Growing pains

Like anything that grows, your comfort zone has to overcome the forces that will stunt it. Being crippled with indecision is one way to stunt growth (but what I learned was the more I grew my comfort zone, the more confident my decision making became). Having unsupportive people around you is another (people who want to keep you very firmly stuck in your smaller zone, not because they are bad, but because often someone else's bravery reminds them of their own fear). Fear, of course, is a major obstacle to growth, be that financial, dread of criticism, fear of failure, not knowing enough or being good enough, fear of change or asking for help. These stunts are there for everyone, but just like body fitness only comes to those who stretch themselves and understand a certain amount of discomfort is part of the process, so emotional growth only comes to those who understand these are natural reactions, accepting uncomfortable feelings like fear as part of the process, not a reason not to do it. Imagine what you would do if you didn't need anyone's approval? What would you try if no one saw you fall on your face? What would you want if you didn't have to justify it to someone else? What would you do for yourself if you didn't want to not upset people around you?

This mid-age is like no other in history. A fixed mindset will think mid-age is the end of youth, no point in changing now. A growth mindset will see mid-age as the amazing potential it is. What I say next is the most important lesson of this book.

> ***It's the difference between saying 'I'll grow old gracefully' and 'Fuck it, I want to grow powerfully.'***

Adopting the mindset that trying and maybe even failing is good for us takes a bit of convincing. Looking silly, not being good at something, being a learner again can feel a bit ugly, and we just want life to be pretty. But a vibrant midlife isn't interested in pretty; it wants character. Designers, engineers, scientists, business people all get better by failing and trying again, learning from experience and improving next time. Failed expectations don't mean you're a failure; it may mean the expectation was wrong, or it might mean you learned something.

I had a fear of cold water. A visceral hatred. I told myself I just 'wasn't one of those people' who could tolerate cold water. But the sea is like a plug socket to me, an energy source that boosts me up. I swam every chance I got in warm waters, yet for years, on wild west coast of Ireland holidays, I pottered at the edge while my girls whooped in the waves. One day, while I was staying at a creative retreat in the Irish midlands, I followed my fellow guests to the stunning Lake Annamakerrig on the grounds. These wonderful women would shake off their creative cobwebs every day, delving into the deep dark glacial water, emerging with something akin to that glow from the old Ready Brek ads of my childhood. I could literally think of nothing worse than plunging into that freezing purgatory. But, I'd been growing. I'd been challenging my beliefs. I'd been exploring my authentic potential and so one day, I stripped off my clothes and in my bra and knickers, walked into the water. I felt that I had been through so much internal pain, no amount of external pain could affect me. Taking a deep breath, I pictured myself already in the water, bypassing my brain's bug by already seeing it into reality, and slipped forward. The frigid shock took my breath away, I won't lie. My body spasmed with the searing cold. But then something miraculous happened. I didn't die. I wasn't in pain. I was enveloped in the stunning cold and it was nothing short of euphoric. I emerged reluctantly, expecting the cold air to lacerate me. But the Ready Brek glow protected me and as I squelched back to my room,

I knew I was changed. Not because I was now 'one of those people', but because I'd opened up a doorway in my life that nothing but my own beliefs had kept locked. Later that summer, in the wild Atlantic soothing sea of Donegal, I became a mermaid. I dived into the waves and swam through the green salty sea, so intrinsically connected to nature, away from the shore I had loitered on for so many years afraid of the discomfort of the cold, never imagining the bliss that lay beyond.

Growth is learning to sit more comfortably with uncomfortable feelings like fear, resistance, embarrassment. Like leaping into the cold, stark sea, you realise you can bear much more discomfort than you think. A feeling is just a feeling. It will pass. But the growth comes in feeling it, allowing it to tell you something, and then pushing through. In doing so you are also rewiring neurological connections in your brain so it becomes easier and easier to do.

> ***Learning to notice your feelings more, understanding your gut instinct more, listening to yourself more, means becoming more aware. That's a big growth spurt right there. And being more self-aware is the crux of it all.***

You also start to become more aware of moments of happiness, joy and contentment. Those delicious feelings, the glories, the pride, the moments of satisfaction, of just being and knowing, that in this moment, you are fucking alive and OK. The more feelings you're aware of, the more you'll become aware of. Yes, you feel the uncomfortable feelings but also the comfortable ones. Sparking joy is contagious. Just ask Marie Kondo. The more you feel it, the more you might think about what is causing it. What is giving me energy? Who is making me feel lighter? What leaves me enthused? What inspires me? What makes me feel so fucking good I do a little dance in the kitchen? When you stop to take notice of the feeling, you also connect with what caused it. And when you know what causes you to feel engaged, motivated, loved, valued, joyous, happy, silly in a 'I might just break into dance' way, then you can start to figure out how to create a life that is pulsing with them. This is growth. Being prepared to understand the discomfort will also have an upside. Asking questions, challenging the routines you live on autopilot, demanding proof on self-limiting beliefs that only serve to hold you back, all of this is growth. Instead of hovering wishy washy at the edge, I am able to dive into the cold dark waters, a mermaid. A frickin' mermaid! I'd always been afraid of cold water but now I was not only taking a leap of faith in myself by taking a leap into the cold Atlantic sea, I experienced a whoop of glory I could never have imagined. That whoop of glory was the soft sound of my comfort zone stretching.

Growing means you stand taller

I feel I have grown more in the last few years than at any time since I left formal education. I pushed myself to date again as a mid-aged, single parenting woman, go back to college, learn a new sport, and build a new business. I've had 'aha' moments, breakthrough moments, painful repositioning moments, and wonderful shattering of limiting-beliefs moments. The best decision I ever made in a lifetime of billions of decisions was standing on my dad's doorstep with a pus-infected abscess, choosing to stop stagnating, and grow; to challenge myself, because I knew from the pain of overcoming the challenges life had thrown me the previous few years, that I could survive challenges. The decision I made to thrive, not just survive this one wild and precious life, as poet Mary Oliver calls it. The decision to stop sinking into the drama of external elements, and grow towards, and into, the adventure of my own life. To embrace growth and all its discomfort as an intrinsic part of happiness.

My thirty-year-old self would hardly recognise my fifty-year-old self. My thirty-year-old self believed she was capable of so many things, had achieved so many things, but she also believed she was a 10km runner, wasn't sporty, hated cold water, and wanted to be a writer but couldn't be. There wouldn't have been enough psychedelic drugs to let my forty-year-old self, crushed and overwhelmed with shock from parent-care, child-care and a devastating marriage, imagine who she could become.

My forty-five-year-old self, shattered by the wrecking ball of the death of a parent and the end of a marriage, would not recognise the fifty-year-old who rented a lit-up dance floor for her milestone birthday and danced with an amazing tribe of family and friends to celebrate: now a marathon veteran, sea swimming mermaid, yoga-loving, windsurfing, author, graduate, business owner, life coach; a life enhanced by philosophy and psychology and growing. *None of that* my forty-year-old would have recognised. What will my next ten and twenty years have in store? Grief, loss, frustration, disappointment? Of course; they're a natural part of life. Love, adventure, achievement, passion? Yes, because I choose to grow. There is no ceiling, just a wide open sky.

> ***Midlife growing is vital so that your younger self will always be surprised by your older self, and your older self will always be proud and grateful for how your younger self chose to live.***

We stunt our growth with phrases like:

'When I'm fitter, I will …'

'When I've lost the weight, I will …'

'When I have more time, I'll …'

The problem is that some of those 'whens' might never come, or they might get delayed so that the 'I wills' become, by default 'I won't's and I didn't's'. (Global pandemic anyone?) That means your potential to grow gets delayed

The opposite of growth is shrinkage, but there is a darker bridge between the two: stagnation. If you stagnate too long in midlife because of the overwhelm, conditioning, loss of identity and confusion, you risk spending years, if not decades, on autopilot. Growth is about releasing the performing circus monkey, who's had all its natural urges tamed, to let it begin to listen to and follow its natural instincts. It's about finding, and then listening to, your inner voice. This doesn't mean always going bigger, higher, faster, more. Growth – real personal growth – can mean deciding on smaller, lower, slower, less. It's whatever your authentic potential for the life you really want to be living means.

Perfection is not the goal; progression is.

Arrival is not the goal; evolution is.

Ticking boxes and living life by default is not the goal; intentionally living and exploring your authentic potential is.

Despite the extra decades, never settle for a life half lived, because you don't know how long the other half is. Don't put aside your happiness and fulfilment until you've cleared the dishes or sent the email; don't postpone being the person you want to be until you've lost a few pounds. Be her today. Tomorrow's you will thank you.

Decision #3 – My MidLife Growth Chart

Either print off the Growth Chart at www.themidlifecoach.org/midliferedefined/resources or simply draw a vertical line down your page. Instead of marking it with height measurements, mark out decades: 10, 20, 30, 40, 50, 60, 70, 80, 90. Draw a line at your current age. Fill in the sections before that line in blocks of colour – childhood, education, travel, further education, career. Mark off the headline stuff – graduating, a loss, a gain, maybe getting married, buying a home, winning a tournament, having a child, getting a promotion. Fill that first section with marks of all the things that have happened in your life. Add in the ones that maybe wouldn't make the headlines, but they mattered: that holiday, that unexpected moment of happiness; stages where you have really pushed your comfort zone, or achieved something – when you sat exams, when you practised and competed at a sport. It might be when you became a parent, went for a promotion, asked for a raise. When you overcame a major challenge or when you got through a difficult situation. It's yours to play with. Come at it with joy.

Now look at the space that is left. Mark any headlines you know about … a child graduating or leaving school, retirement, holiday or trip planned. Make a list of all the things you want to happen in this time. Every single dream. Every little and large aspiration, from a Michelin star meal to a degree. Create the boxes, big and small, you want to check off. Take your time. Leave it somewhere you'll see it every day and add to it as you put on your makeup, or reach for the milk or boil the kettle. Build it up. Flesh it out. Create. Challenge. Commit. Aspire. Inspire.

Mark things you would like to learn, accomplish, overcome, try, forgive, forge ahead with, begin, find, see, travel to, experience. Really, really try not to rationalise yourself out of any of them. Let yourself go. No one is forcing you to sign a contract committing you to anything.

What would you do if you weren't afraid?

What would you do if you weren't worried about what anyone else thought?

What would you try if you believed you could do it?

Go back to your Wheel of Life, and ask what would I be doing if my life was more balanced?

You don't have to be specific about where you make the marks, and you don't have to think you'll do every single one. You are just building a growth chart of possibility and designing a reality where you are open to growing, right until the end of this one wild and precious life.

9

BECAUSE I'M *Worth It*

★

INVESTMENT

The most important decision in midlife is the one to invest in yourself by signing your own permission slip. Invest money certainly, but not necessarily. Invest your time, energy, thoughts, focus, light, strengths, compassion, curiosity, imagination, your mind, body and soul on yourself. That is one of the most important advantages that we women of this magnificent midlife generation have been given – even though it still feels risky, or subverted. Investment is making sure the light you shine on so many other people gets turned back on yourself too.

As I started connecting to my mind, I also realised I'd disconnected from my body. Once the vehicle I'd glided through life on, it had become something that almost belonged to other people. Between marriage, maternity and menopausal whisperings, my connection to self had taken a sabbatical. So in the spirit of growth and investment, I did two things. Research had already shown me that midlife is a critical time for women to build strength, and yoga and pilates are ideal for this. Yoga in particular really began to connect my mind to my body, with breathing as the bridge. For the first time in a long time, I felt completely at one with myself. The second thing I did was slightly more drastic. I flew to Argentina to learn tango.

Let me be completely honest. I'm not a dancer (oh look, limiting belief!). I mean, I'm not someone who has been told 'hey babe, your rhythm is off the charts!' I dance in my kitchen and I let rip at gigs, but step-orientated dance has always been a challenge. Years ago, my friend Carol and I went on holiday to Cuba and booked salsa classes beforehand so we could go dancing in Havana. Let's just say, light of feet and rhythmic of hips, I was not. So I wasn't going to Buenos Aires to become a tango expert. I went because I was writing about women losing their sense of sensuality, and tango apparently is one of the places to find it. Tango is connecting with yourself. You have to close your eyes, let go of control and trust your body to react simultaneously to the lead's movements. This sounded like the opposite of comfortable but the kids were spending Easter with their dad, so I was footloose and fancy free. Well, foot clumsy and fancy free. It was such an investment of time and money, I nearly cancelled a hundred times. But I knew that learning to dance in a strange sultry country was really about finding my feet again. When I got there, I bought glamorous blue tango shoes, had lessons with wonderful teachers and even found myself blindfolded in a strange man's apartment (not a Tinder date gone wrong. Or gone right, depending on your perspective). He was a Tango Psychologist. Argentine tango has long been used as a therapy for neurological disorders, including depression and stress, because it involves total trust in self, learning to surrender to the moment, be present and connected to your body and music. And so I found myself blindfolded and disorientated, soul-searing music playing all around me. I could feel him behind me, breathing softly. Then I felt him touch my forearm. I turned towards the touch and lifted my arm. 'Don't move your head or your body, just the part I touch,' he corrected me gently. He touched my calf with what I presume was his shin. I tried to keep still except for moving my lower leg. 'Relax, breathe, don't think, and just move as I tap an area.' He had a very soothing voice so I started to relax, focusing on my breathing, absorbing the music, and slowly the exercise began to take shape. As soon as I stopped trying to predict where he would tap me next, I became less jerky. I raised my arm, turned my shoulder, lifted my foot, extended my leg and as he got faster, my movements became more flowing. I realised I was completely in tune with my body and the music, with no thought in the process. That is the art of tango. It isn't about set steps, it's about total surrender, letting go so that there is only you, the music and the subtle prompts of your partner's body, your body responding almost simultaneously to his steps forward or backwards. There can be no thinking. For someone like me who had thoughts on top of her thoughts, this was a mind-fuck. This was the moment, in a stranger's apartment, in a strange city, that I understood that I could survive without being controlled by my thoughts. It would be the start of months and then years of learning how to practise letting go, becoming aware of my thoughts rather than thinking I am my thoughts.

At last he took my hand and led me to the middle of the room. 'Let us dance.'

I was still blindfolded. When you dance the tango, your arms are raised just below your shoulders, one hand on his shoulder, the other hand in his. Cheek to cheek, not face to face. Your chests are close, the beat of the music a heartbeat between you. Everything depends on the female partner relaxing, committing to listening to her body, allowing all her energy to follow the hints of movement provided by the male-performing partner. I'd been watching couples dance in the Milonga halls the nights before, amazed by the rapture on their faces. Not the pompous look of the rose-between-teeth caricatures you see on TV. This was the rapture of being in complete tune with your body, your thoughts given the night off. There is a phrase for this rapture: tangasm. I remember watching one couple, most likely in their sixties or even seventies. The look of rapture on their eyes-closed faces; they looked so in love my heart melted. Until the dance ended and they went off to different tables, and brought back new partners. Again, they began to dance, and again the same face of rapture. I realised then, the dance isn't about loving your partner, it's about loving the experience of being at one with yourself.

I stood blinded, yet seeing how important it was to let my thoughts quieten so that my body could step into the space, waiting for his first movement: a step back, a step forward, or even a step to the side. I'd spent three days of lessons predicting every step and therefore usually getting it wrong. 'Don't predict,' my lovely and patient teacher Raoul would smile. 'Let go and flow.' Easier said than done when you're as uptight and bruised as I was. Holding on was the only thing keeping me going, I wanted to tell him!

But this time, blindfolded, unable to see myself and partner in the mirrored walls of the dance studio, I waited for the lovely pause at the beginning of each dance when you gently sway as a couple until you are in tune, before he takes his first step. I swayed and waited. And as he moved (forward as it happens), my body responded before my mind could make a decision. It wasn't perfect, I predicted too many steps, but it was a complete improvement on previous dances. It wasn't about trusting the partner. It was about trusting myself. It was a seismic shift in my relationship with myself. I had two, maybe three tangasms that week. Fleeting feelings of rapture when I let go enough to surrender to the music, to the partner, and to myself. It was the beginning of a reacquaintance with who I am, my relationship with my body and my mind after years of feeling disconnected. The door had opened. I had invested in myself, and I will never, ever shortchange myself again. Now I dance in my kitchen, do yoga, swim in the sea, and try as much as possible to listen to my body and all of its messages as much, if not more, than the thoughts in my head.

Society conditions us to believe that IQ is the most important quality. But really, finding balance between your IQ, your EQ (emotional intelligence) and your BQ (body intelligence) is what connects you with yourself.

Investment begins with internal inspiration

We often think of inspiration as coming from external triggers. This external inspiration is a really important part of our growth by seeing what can be achieved, and realising we might be able to do or be something similar. But there is another inspiration, and it comes from within. We are very good at negative self-talk and self-criticism, and not so good at self-praise and being awed by ourselves. In Section 1 you began to explore and discover more about yourself because while you often look to others for inspiration, inspiring yourself is a dynamic and productive way of pushing through change. To a lot of women, being inspired by yourself feels counterintuitive because you're taught that Good Girls are self-depreciating and modest. Self-investment means moving from self-flagellation to self-focus. Being inspired by yourself does not involve walking around with an 'I'm fabulous' tattoo on your forehead. Being self-inspired means listening to your own voice. Not the one saying 'I should' but the one saying 'I could' and 'I can' and 'I want' and 'I need'.

It means paying attention to what's making you tick, what's energising you, and then living intentionally. It's letting your mind explore an idea rather than immediately shutting it down because you're too busy, too overwhelmed or too scared. It's about not believing the belief we were handed as young girls, that taking time out for ourselves is selfish. It's about stopping asking who am I supposed to be, and learning who you actually are and want to be.

You can tell yourself you aren't sporty, or you can start being sporty, one walk, one run, one fitness class at a time. You can tell yourself you are only worthy when you have a partner, or you can start valuing yourself today, taking charge of your own life, buying a vibrator if you so desire, but not waiting for someone else to give you permission to be living (or have an orgasm). You can tell yourself you are too long in the tooth to start a new career or take up a new passion, or you can slightly shift your perspective and see a woman in her prime, ready and able to do anything she damn well wants. (The number of clients I've had who have started a whole new life or career in their fifties and sixties is testament to this). Remember you have an extra two or three decades, and most of the standard boxes have already been ticked. This is the time to imagine new boxes to tick. To think outside the boxes completely.

> ***No generation of women have ever had this mid-age before so you get to define what it can be.***

There is nothing like getting out of your own way, expanding your comfort zone and pushing yourself into a place where what was once discomfort is now your comfort zone. Inspiration begins within and flows out.

Remember when you were a child and you played roles you saw in the adult world? Astronauts, doctors, vets, pop stars, nurses, hairdressers, sports champions, teachers, shop assistants, farmers, musicians, beauticians, TV presenters, chefs? Every one of those imaginative games was driven by a spark of interest that that role ignited in your young self as you tried it on for size. Then, remember when you were an awkward, rapidly evolving, ever-mind-changing, impression-absorbing teenager? The endless passions and problems that weaved their way through your worries and wants; your style changing with the weather, certain music seeing you like no human in your life could? For many of those sparks of interest, you might have become 'too cool' or they became too 'not for girls' according to external pressures, and fell by the wayside.

Remember then how those array of potential sparks were funnelled down through education, slowly neglected, abandoned or narrowed until you went from lots of interests to a few, from several sports to one, when you went from maybe ten subjects down to three, specialising further in a degree or course? All of those sparks filtered through a funnel until your life was narrowed and focused. Of course you have to concentrate on particular areas, because you can't live all of those lives at once, that movie being called *Revolving Doors* rather than *Sliding Doors*.

But what happened to those sparks? They're still there. But perhaps you became afraid of the feelings or repercussions. Or naturally, a life of responsibilities took over. What I felt myself, and what I see so often in the women I coach, is that I, and they, want more from life than just doing. We want to be more of our core, and less the outer doll. This can feel confusing because we feel our lives are already bursting at the seams, and cannot possibly fit in another 'thing'. You may feel like slightly dying, but in fact those feelings are the opposite of dying; they are the burning embers of sparks desperate to come alive. Inspiration comes from your thoughts on the past, present and future; inspiration that can kill or thrill you.

Past pleasures and cultural handcuffs

Your sense of self comes from what energises you, yet it's easy to align your identity to external investments that you have no control over

– people, fashions, expectations, money. When you look back at the moments when you've inspired yourself, they're usually not because of a handbag, but hard work, patience, curiosity, generosity, learning, yearning for something. The role models you had when you didn't know as much as you do now may not be the ones you need now. Like most teenagers, I never considered my parents role models at the time. Mum wasn't changing the world like BBC war correspondent Kate Adie who was (and still is) my role model. But when I gave my mum's eulogy, I realised that the things she valued most – family, friends and being demonstrative with her love – made her my most important role model, just as I now see my dad role models a capacity to never stop learning. The first time I did coaching, I was asked to list the positives I got from my parents which really made me think, since we spend much of our early life bitching about all the things we hate about them! Questioning those too is important as we decide which we want to keep and which we want to ditch.

I look at the tribe of friends I've built from the various stages of my life. They are so different yet they all, in some form or other, represent an aspect of me. Some have botox, some never wear makeup; some share my love of gin and wine, others barely drink; some are loud and dramatic, some are thoughtful and shy; some are ignited by latest fashions, others couldn't give two hoots what they wear. They are all glorious and they all inspire me.

Western culture often gives women two beliefs that hold us back. The first is that we are indispensable (because our role as mother/daughter/partner/colleague defines us) and the second is that we have no right to put our own needs first. Redefining midlife means ditching the extra pounds by ditching the dead weight on your shoulders instead. Ditch the grandiose ideas of your mother that you're the only one who can do things right. Ditch the martyrdom of your mother that you don't deserve as big a helping on the plate as everyone else at the table. Ditch the criticism of your father that you're 'too'. Ditch the rejection of that early lover that you weren't perfect. Ditch it all, and show up as worthy of the same investment you give to others. Your midlife mission is to turn your light firmly back on yourself and shine in your own right, whatever that means for you.

The presence of mind

The best investment you can make for yourself is to take back control of your thoughts and actions, switch off autopilot and live as intentionally as you possibly can. You're worried about bills without realising you have bankrupted yourself by giving so much of yourself away for free, leaving you broke and broken. That doesn't mean sitting cross legged and muttering 'Om' while the world burns around you; it means deciding with intent how *you* want to live your day, and from there manage all your responsibilities. It means asking are you, in this moment, below or above the line.

> ***It's about choosing who you are; not being told who you are.***

Take something as simple as breathing. How often do you struggle for a deep breath? Several times in my life, I've had panic attacks, the struggle for breath the most frightening experience I've ever had. Yet we're not taught how to breathe. Only through yoga have I learned how to breathe properly, now treasuring and actioning deep and loving breaths whether it's my first conscious breath in the morning, during my yoga practice or just a check-in moment through the day. Take nature. When I was a child growing up being dragged on endless 'walks', I just assumed my parents were a bit touched. Who would 'walk' somewhere without going anywhere? Then as I matured and might actually have appreciated how sunlight glints on grass, I was too busy STRIVING, ACHIEVING and JUGGLING. In my favourite book, *The Color Purple*, Sis ponders how anyone can walk past the colour purple and not be grateful to God. I don't have a god but I am spiritual and so grateful to Mother Nature every time I see purple, and new snowdrops defeating winter. If that's ageing, I'm all for it. I now take inspiration from the world I'm walking in, my trees, the blossoms, the birds. I couldn't give two figs what my fig and feta salad looks like on Instagram but OMG look at the heron! Investing in myself means living in the moment as much as I can and being aware of what gives me joy. Of trying to stay above the line so I am living by my design.

One of the ways we lose control of the moment is by dwelling on past actions and hurts, or wishing things were different. But you have no control in those areas. A technique I use is called CIA. No, we're not calling in the Feds. This is about frisking your mind, not your body. So to CIA something you look at what you can Control, what you can Influence, and what you have to Accept. You don't have to like what needs to be accepted (and often won't), but the quicker you leave the space of trying to change something you can't, the quicker you get back into your areas of control and influence. Accepting what you can't change means you control and influence your response. Even if you are living the life of your dreams, things will happen to upset it, causing you pain and discomfort. Just look at the 2020 global pandemic. Even without the big external events, you'll likely encounter something every day that is not in your plan. Accepting what you can't control as quickly as possible (basically everything except your thoughts and actions), and getting back to how you can influence and control the rest of the day will keep you empowered, and dare I say, inspired.

One of the worst expectations we absorb is that somehow we are meant to be happy all of the time. But we are part of nature. And as anyone who has watched any David Attenborough knows, nature is both beautiful and brutal. One of the things I coach my clients is that the goal is not 100% happiness but an ability to live with a wide range of emotions, comfortable and uncomfortable. If you hang your happiness on something out of your control, you set yourself up for pain. Happiness is a multi-faceted concept. We mostly think of happiness as the experience – the dopamine hit. While those happiness hits are important, there are two other types of happiness that require a bit more commitment. The second type of happiness comes from personal growth and development. You might not be happy during the experience, but later you know it has somehow made your life better. Spending five years travelling from my kids in Dublin to my mum in Belfast every other weekend was brutal. But the experience of discovering just how far I can push myself, of hurting so bad I might (and did) break, of giving my mum the care and then death she deserved, is one of the greatest gifts of my life. Training for and running a marathon wasn't a barrel of laughs. I was in physical pain. Often. And that was just the recommended ice baths after a long run to ease my muscles. But the happiness I have from that experience will stay with me forever.

The third type of happiness is the value you get from contribution, purpose, positively impacting others, feeling that you matter. Making an impact NOT to the detriment of your needs and integrity, but from a place of strength and intention. Your midlife design needs to have a balance of these three types of happiness. It's not about the handbag you carry; it's about the baggage you dump.

The future is bright

Forget age. Those numbers of forty, fifty and sixty are arbitrary. They don't mean anything any more. The only age that matters is the age you finally own your shit. Every generation of women has slowly evolved women's quality of life, but this generation is completely redefining middle age in a way the teenagers of the 1950s redefined children. I look at my mum and the life she might have lived if she had been given permission. I look at the generations of women before us who never had the chance to explore their potential. Sometimes we have to take inspiration from the people who couldn't have what we can, and invest in ourselves in a way they could never have done. And then we have to become role models for the generations to come.

In his 2019 book, *The Happiness Curve*, researcher Jonathan Rauch found that once conditions such as income, employment, health and marriage are factored out of the equation, life satisfaction declines from our early twenties until we hit our fifties. Then it turns around and rises, right through midlife. This pattern has been found in countries and cultures around the world; a version of it has even been detected in chimpanzees and orang utans. We assume (mostly because of the militant anti-ageing propaganda) that ageing is a bad thing and therefore will make us miserable. But instead, ageing fights happiness until midlife, then switches sides. Ageing is obviously never the only thing going on and our life satisfaction at any given time will depend on many things; but the independent effect of ageing is more than enough to make a noticeable positive difference, especially if the rest of your life is stable and smooth. The myth that at fifty our best years are behind us is one of the biggest causes of discontent because we assume that if we're not fulfilled at fifty, we never will be. In fact, the happiness curve shows that, all things being equal, the best of life is yet to come. From that point, ageing makes us more positive, and less stressed and regretful.

The things I have achieved DESPITE ageing, and DESPITE trauma and grief have been life enhancing. I feel that this is the time I'm glowing and growing the most (notwithstanding the challenges and responsibilities that midlife hurls at us at record-breaking force). I finally give less fucks about stuff that isn't actually important and more fucks about me and how I want my life to feel. But it takes intentional investment. It is never too late to invest in yourself: your body, your mind, your *peace* of mind, your creativity, your health, your career, your joy, your pleasure, your passions, your interests, your adventures. It is a daily commitment.

The false assumption that we will have peaked by middle age not only makes us miserable, it stops us striving to grow and evolve. That stereotype of the midlife crisis is just not borne out. Societal recourse and reality are at odds. We're not becoming de-sexualised; we're seeing more and more women in their fifties, sixties and even seventies on TV being vibrant sexual beings. We're not fading into the background, redundant; one of the largest cohorts of people setting up businesses is women aged fifty plus. Instead of falling apart, we're more likely to be strengthening up – the female upsurge in pilates/yoga/running/football/cycling is a testament to that. We're not being devalued: non-nubile celebrities such as Winona Ryder, Susan Sarandon, Helen Mirren, Diane Keaton, and Jane Fonda are being used by leading designers in advertising, and playing leading women in movies. Female leaders all over the world are changing the world. Yet you would never guess this from the way we often still think and talk about ageing.To invest in yourself, you can look for inspiration rather than intimidation to live a life that energises you rather than drains you. You can keep intentional about how you want to live. You don't have to love your wrinkles, but you do have to accept them and then not let them hold you back. Body image is a trend; don't let a trend dictate your self-worth. Instead, be inspired by those who feel comfortable in their own skin, whether they're wearing Christian Louboutins or crocs. Can you imagine how it must have been to be a poor, and therefore scrawny woman, a hundred years ago when chubby, bellied women were deemed beautiful because it meant they were rich? Expectations are not real. It's fashion.

In our twenties we talked a lot about who we fancied and wanted to love. In our thirties we talked a lot about our children. Now, it's time to talk about ourselves.

We each of us never stop having the potential we had from our childhood. Midlife is a time for us to let that potential become more powerful. Nothing is more inspiring than that.

Decision # 4 – Happiness roadmap

Go back and look at your Growth Chart. Look at some of the experiences you marked in your life to date, and what you have included in your life ahead. Can you split them into three categories of happiness?

- ★ Experiences and feelings of joy
- ★ Personal growth/expanded comfort zone
- ★ Contribution

Try to add more to the second and third columns. Flesh it out. Your growth chart will grow as you continue on with this book, as your mind opens to more and more potential, you will keep adding things you want for yourself, big and small, headliners and tiny changes, habits and holidays, more and less.

10

YES, *I Fucking Can!*

★

COURAGE

Other people's lives are a bit like Facebook – we often only see the finished product – the success, the sunrise, the laughing family, the good news. There are plenty of days and moments that never make it onto Facebook and Instagram stories, yet those moments are no less important. When I wrote my first book, I constantly worried that it wasn't good enough. But having gone through the process of messy first drafts, endless edits and redrafts with advice from professionals, until the final published book resembled a long lost cousin of the original draft, I can relax more with my writing. I now know the first draft just has to be written, not perfect. The key is progress, not perfection. Look back on a time when you surprised yourself with success. It probably started with a fear of failure, or a belief that it couldn't happen, and then a few hits and misses. My marathon training was a long process of stops and starts and it's not the medal I remember, it's the overcoming fear, the failures but starting again, the expanding my comfort zone with every new run. I will mentally benefit from that training long after my muscle memory has faded and the abs have been enveloped in Gin Girth. When we make an assumption that fear is always a bad thing, we're wrong.

It's the fear of fear that hurts us.

Fear itself is a primary survival technique, but there are actually two types of fear. *Survival* fear is about surviving. *Growth* fear stops us thriving. Survival fear is our body and mind's natural warning to real dangers so that we react without thinking to survive. *Growth* fear doesn't want us to change because our brains are wired to resist it because the status quo is safer. So every positive change you make you have to intentionally step over the trip wire of fear and have courage. When you experience a feeling like fear, anger, or discomfort it's not because you are a failure, it's because you are alive.

Fearing failure is the failure (courage is the success, regardless of the outcome)

Every one of us fails. Every single one of us. We 'fail' at the big things and we 'fail' at thousands of little things every day.

We only see the Facebook happy.

We only see the Twitter angry.

But EVERYONE loses their way. Stop looking at them. YOU are your compass.

Everyone feels fear. Everyone. Some people let it stop them, and other people take a deep breath and plunge through it.

There is only one way to expand your comfort zone: by stepping out of it and pulling the circumference in around you. It takes courage to be your full size when told to be smaller, to speak up when told to keep quiet, to say 'this is me' when told to be something else, to explain what is important to you when told women's issues are less important. There is trauma in not being heard. There is trauma in not being understood. There is trauma in not being seen. There is trauma in feeling you somehow need permission to follow your desires. There is trauma in being afraid to be yourself. There is trauma in thinking your only value is what you do for others. There is trauma in being held hostage to fear. There is trauma in living half a life. Finding and using your courage is the only way to start healing that trauma.

Getting comfortable with discomfort

When I was a kid, I loved the film *Jaws*. When I say loved it, I mean I loved hiding behind the sofa and screaming. Its brilliance was in the expectation – the sinister fin gliding silently through the water; it's what I couldn't see that scared me the most. Years later I read that a young Steven Spielberg couldn't afford a realistic shark, so focused instead on the fin and the suspense it created. When you finally see the shark as it chomps the boat in two, it's the un-scariest shark you've ever seen! What Spielberg created was fear of the fear which was much more intense. I take the same view of scary emotions now. We avoid them because we fear them. We don't want to feel sad, or angry, or alone. We drink, overeat, watch too much TV, do too much internet shopping. Anything to avoid looking emotions in the face. The fins go on circling us. But here's the thing. Emotions are like that plastic shark. When you look them in the face, you can see that they aren't really going to bite your legs off. Sure, they might look a little bit scary, but it is your fear of them that gives them the power. As I grew, I was able to see that all the times I'd seen the circling fins in my life for what they really were, I had survived. When I jump into the cold waves, knowing there will be several seconds of thrilling, terrifying discomfort, it is because I know there is no physical pain as bad as the emotional pains I have survived. I can lunge into freezing water because I have survived holding one of the people I love most in my life as they took their last breath. I can push through the agony of birthing a new business, because I have survived the agony of losing babies. I can run a mental marathon because I know that success is not the medal; success is the metal in my mind.

I have walked through fucking fire. So many women I know as friends or have coached have walked through fire. It's not the burning that changes our lives; it's surviving the flames. It is the rising from those flames. I'm sure you can think of at least one time in your life when you thought you wouldn't get through it. But you did. Emotions are there to be felt, yet emotions are the things we were told to keep in check. You need to make sure those you love understand your emotions are valid, and only when you acknowledge them can you make an intentional choice of how to respond to them. You have to sit in the flames of your emotions and know you can withstand the heat.

Yet we think if we're sad, we're a failure. That we're only meant to feel happy and anything else needs to be suppressed. Being taught that being angry or frustrated is bad, we never stood a chance. 'Give us a smile, love,' we were repeatedly told. Ambition and anger did not accessorise us as well as a pretty smile and a flick of the hair. If there is one thing the Covid-19 pandemic has taught us it is that getting comfortable with discomfort matters. That when the chips are down, the external shite we normally look to for affirmation doesn't mean a thing.That handbag? Her thighs? Those likes? Not remotely relevant. Liberated from all the external distraction, we can decide who and what really matters and gives us joy. When you turn your light on you, you will glow.

I'm not suggesting you have to go all Eat, Pray, Love. But courage is letting go of crutches – partner, wine, over-exercising, over-eating to stop you feeling the feeling. Unless you feel the feelings, you can't deal with them. Feeling the emotions is not the same as being the emotion. Just like you are not your thoughts, you are not your emotions.There is a lovely Buddhist technique for dealing with emotions that are uncomfortable. I love it because it's called RAIN, which reminds me of my dad telling me you can't always wait for the sun to shine. You have to learn to dance in the rain too.

So when it comes to difficult emotions, here's how to dance in the rain.

R – recognise it. What you resist, persists, so if you pretend it's not really there, or cover it up with too much wine, raiding the fridge, keeping busy, it will only get more intense. Recognise the emotion, call it what it is – fear, shame, self-loathing, sadness, loneliness, resentment. Through the sheer act of saying 'I'm feeling afraid,' the sting is taken out of its tail, and it's easier to manage.

Next is the A – accept it and allow it to be. This might feel dangerous and hard, but even for a few minutes, don't fight it, don't try to fix it. Allow it to be, in a really kind and gentle way for yourself. You are not the emotion, so it's not 'I'm afraid/sad, lonely/frustrated' but 'I'm feeling afraid/sad/lonely/frustrated".

Then it's I – Investigate the reasons for the feeling (and I always feel this is the most powerful one). List the reasons for the feeling, breaking down the fear into one or two specific issues, rather than an umbrella experience. It gives you something to work with. For example, I was afraid of going on a date for the first time in a hundred years. When I really looked at the fear, I realised I was afraid of walking in and being flustered. So I was able to take away that fear by arriving early, going to the bathroom to catch my breath and brush my hair, and then be seated calmly at the table, in control of myself, before my date arrived. I was also afraid of being stuck on a bad date. So I devised a plan in advance in case I needed a quick exit. I had had an umbrella fear of going on a date, but when I really looked at why I was afraid, I was able to mitigate most of it. Then all I had to worry about was how much cleavage to expose ;-)

I had a client who was afraid of pitching her business at meetings. When we really investigated the fear it was actually a fear of feeling unprepared. Now before every meeting she emails the proposal in advance so that she doesn't have to worry about forgetting anything. One sub-plot fear had stopped her carrying out the major plot.

The final part of the RAIN exercise is N – non-identification. Do not mistake the emotion for you. It is a feeling that will pass. It is not you. As I've explained, you are the sky, and your thoughts and feelings are the clouds passing by. Sure, some are dark and heavy and take a while to move on, but move on eventually they do. Dance in the rain until the sun shines again.

*

Courage is not about *not* being afraid. It's about accepting your fear, and moving forward anyway. You can absolutely survive, and even get used to recognising uncomfortable feelings without trying to quell, fix, or excuse them. You're maybe not welcoming them in with open arms, but you are giving them a tentative smile, and saying 'Hello, I'm Denise. You must be shame.'

It's scary. It feels dangerous, but also strangely liberating. You are welcoming all of you into the room, rather than leaving the monsters outside, staring through the window, tapping on the glass, haunting you. You treat your thoughts as guests. I call this the Team Chat. Fear? Come and tell me how you feel. (If you don't let it, it gets very SHOUTY in your brain at 4am). Then let Guilt and Shame have their say. Whatever awkward, scary and uncomfortable feelings and thoughts you might be trying to keep at bay with wine/chocolate/denial, let them have their moment. But now welcome in Wisdom. Bring in all that you know and have experienced to the table. Now Pride – all you have achieved, survived and learned. Now Ambition – what do you want from this situation, relationship, action? Let them all have their say, especially the balances to the negative. When you get to know the feelings a bit better, understand them more, you realise they are all a valid part of you. You might put some music on and dance with them a little, or walk beside them through the park. Maybe, they might eventually take off their disguises, acknowledged and no longer intimidating. Then you get to choose who to bring with you to certain situations, a bit like a plus one. If you don't do this, you're likely going to end up with the default Fear tagging along to everything like a creepy uncle.

> ***Your emotions are valid but they are not the experience. They are only a response to your perception of that experience.***

Remember those self-limiting beliefs? Challenge their source, and seek proof? The same is true of fearful feelings. By just acknowledging and then assessing them, often, they dissipate, or become manageable. By facing your fears, you often find a solution to them.

People pleasing and boundary building

'Fine' is the word of self-abandonment. Many women have a lifetime behind them of abandoning themselves to please others before waking up one morning to precede 'Fine' with that other F word and start living a more honest life. Fuck fine. Fine is a front. It's an affront to how you *really* are. My fine-to-fuck-it moment happened when I found myself externally abandoned by the two tethers that had kept me performing the Dance of Fine, and when I was ready to get up from the rubble, took a deep breath and birthed my first non-fine to begin my life anew. My marriage wasn't what I'd thought, or been led to believe it was. I'd been the cover in many ways, not the content. When I'd tried to express my confusion and unhappiness during the marriage, I was met with denial. I felt my feeling were constantly negated and because I didn't know how to communicate my needs articulately, my external voice got louder and angrier. I shouted because my inner voice was unheard. Honestly? Mostly by me. But now I am louder than I've ever been in my life but I don't have to raise my external voice (well, only when the kids put an empty cranberry juice carton back in the fridge. And the cups. Always the unwashed cups). It takes courage to stop saying fine, realising that all the people you spent the previous couple of decades pleasing, aren't necessarily any more pleased than when you started, and even, dare I say it, a lot more demanding.

Knowing it is one thing however; disrupting the people-pleasing merry-go-round is another. The best way to do this is to set boundaries. I had a client, Noreen, who had a very stressful job in a hospital. She was also the classic Irish Mammy, doing everything for everyone. By the time she came to see me, exhausted, she had realised in all her doing for others, she had forgotten to do her. Just to get a sense of how habitual saying yes had become for her – because we had discovered that saying yes, being helpful and pleasing was how she defined her worth – I asked her to spend a couple of days noting down every yes she gave, from the actual verbal yeses she gave to specific requests, to the unrequested yeses of doing something for others without even being asked (that they could well do themselves). When she took out the (extremely long) list, I asked her to mark them according to drain

(D) or gain (G): which ones had drained her of energy and which ones had given her energy or nourishment. As she realised the D's were beginning to far outweigh the G's, she stopped and looked up at me, her eyes welling with tears. It was that moment that began a transformation in her life. While her top strengths included generosity and kindness, and many of her values centred around caring and doing good, she realised she had used them towards everyone else but herself. And in many cases she realised the perceived kindness wasn't a kindness at all. Constantly disabling a maturing teenager by doing everything for them is not a kindness; enabling them is.

> ***It was only by looking at how many yeses she gave away, did she begin to see that being a people pleaser, and being a kind, valuable person, were not the same thing.***

She began to realise how damaging it was to base her self-worth on being everything to everyone, and made the courageous decision to be more discerning with her yeses. If you realise you are giving away too many yeses, just cross out the ones that make you feel resentful and leave the ones that make you shine.

It's not always easy to listen to your heart, but it's even harder to keep doing something that constantly breaks your heart (or your temper at least).

> ***YES! And yes (sigh) are the same word but the impact of their difference to you is dictionaries apart.***

As a single mum to teenagers, I'm really aware of how I hold myself hostage to the fear that I have to constantly play the bad cop role, and that they'll have more fun with the good cop. When I have to make the hard parenting decisions about phone usage or bedtimes, I tell my girls that I love them so much that I'm prepared to be disliked by them in order to be a good parent and act in their best interest. Equally, I have to also love myself enough not to be held hostage by the fear I might upset others if it's in my best interest. It feels hard because it is hard, breaking a mould.

It's always worth asking – if I say yes to this, what am I saying no to? Then if I say no, what am I saying yes to? This can apply to everything from gathering the collection of cups, glasses and plates that are accumulating in your teenager's bedroom, to not taking on an extra job at work that really isn't your remit.

> ***This is healthy living; unhealthy living is when you have no energy to make your own life work.***

Don't ever feel bad for standing up for yourself and expressing your needs. Having boundaries and sticking to them does not make you a selfish person, it means you have integrity. You cannot be resentful of people not respecting your worth, when you don't respect your worth. You can't be upset when people don't respect your time, if you don't respect your time. Sometimes the most loving thing you can do is set a limit. 'No' is a complete sentence. Add a smile, and it's a fucking story with you as the main character. Stop doing what isn't working. It might feel more comfortable to keep saying yes because it feels less risky, but it's futile. This is why, often the dark side of the people pleaser explodes after a period of time because they give and give but feel unseen and unheard. The reason isn't because people aren't appreciating them (they may, or may not). The reason is they haven't been hearing or seeing what matters to themselves. I've worn that T-shirt and it makes me look like shit. My fear of not being liked often made me do things I didn't want to. It's still an active choice I have to repeatedly make, but now I want me to like me more than the other person likes me. Mostly. (Remember I'm all about progress now not perfection.)

I say the following within the obvious context that we love our kids above all else. But we give them enough. Providing food and hugs is likely enough. It's time to give to ourselves too. We can disable them by doing too much for them. They need to grow, make mistakes, learn their own lessons.

When I try to be everything to everyone, I think of my mum. Then I think about the opportunities in my life that she never had. And then I look at my three girls and I remember that I want to be a role model to them. Do I want them to grow up thinking they have no right to strive for their own growth and nourishment, because their role is to invest in and nourish all others first? No, I don't. I want them to thrive in this life, not just survive it. I want to be a role model, not a rule book or a rag doll. I want them to recognise I am human, admit my faults, explain my expletives, be adventurous, courageous and kind, and show them how important your friends and passions are, by investing time with those friends and passions. I've heard so many women say they gave their life to their children but now they're gone, why did they give so much? The kids never asked for it, and rarely appreciate it. Setting your boundaries helps you decide what you are prepared to give.

Boundaries are simply physical, emotional and mental limits you put around behaviours, expectations and relationships to protect yourself from being overwhelmed, used or abused. Boundaries might feel a bit scary, as if you are drawing up a border between countries and demanding passports at checkpoints. But really, it is a level of behaviour or respect you have decided is your limit regarding an issue, and once it is clearly articulated, it is up to the other person to adhere or break it. If they break it, there is no need for you to rant and rave. You simply carry out what you said you would when articulating the boundary. It is a relief to know that you don't have to tolerate something that really annoys or upsets you but that if someone continues to overstep your boundary, that is on them. (Easier said than done, I know.)

Communicate clearly. Healthy boundaries aren't meant to punish; they're meant to be mutually beneficial because everyone knows where they stand. How people respond to or respect boundaries isn't a reason to get defensive. It's a great way to figure out how someone really thinks of you. Teenagers of course are going to push your boundaries any which way they can. I've had to train myself not to be swayed by the demonic tantrums that can ensue when the agreed phone time cutoff is reached, because the fight will be much harder next time. Let them have their tantrum, slam the door, rage against the rule. It is so hard. But if I believe it's right, then I have to hunker down through the storm. (Not all the time. Sometimes I'm too tired and I rage back. It's not pretty, but that's life. Progress, not perfection). Visualise your boundaries getting crossed and imagine how you'll handle those situations. This way, when a moment like this comes up, you'll be less likely to dive below the line, hijacked by your emotions.You'll be able to handle it more rationally, above the line. Building boundaries takes time and practice. Again, it is a constant decision. It is hard, but the goal is not perfection. The goal is practice and progress.

Communicating your boundaries and your needs is your job (isn't everything?). Uncommunicated expectations are never met. If you're like me, you have all these ideas of what you expect from someone, and then host a bellyful of resentment when they aren't met. You assume because YOU have thought them, they are transported by osmosis to your partner, child, friend, colleague, hairdresser. You have to name what you want. My client Nicola was working with me because her two sons were now adults, although living at home. She wanted to figure out how to get some life back for herself after years of feeling overwhelmed managing a family, while also running a business with her husband. After some self-discovery work, she was fired up and beginning to design how she wanted her life to feel. However she came to one session in a fume, upset that she still had all the work to do in the home, and no one could see that she wanted more time for herself.

"Have you told them?" I asked her.

She looked at me blankly. "I live in a house with three other adults! Why do they still expect me to do everything?"

Believe me, I could weep sometimes with the hurt of not being seen in my own home, resentful that my teens haven't spontaneously realised it's dinner time and left their Snapchat chats to come down and set the table. As I write that sentence I am, of course, laughing. Of course they're not! Unless I communicate what I expect, it's unlikely to happen. (It's still unlikely to happen but that's a different conversation.) Nicola's family are so embedded in the old paradigm, they haven't noticed that she is shifting her priorities. Of course they're not automatically realising the family dynamic has changed and she no longer has to play the 'mother role' to the extent she did for as long as they can remember. So we worked on ways she could communicate with them that actually, as a family they have entered a new stage: four adults equally sharing the workload. Then it's all about setting your boundaries and clinging on to them for dear life.

Your right to thrive, not just survive

Midlife is a bit like adolescence without the acne and aching lack of confidence. New thoughts and impulses start firing up in your head, but you just need to find a way to channel them. Midlife is also the time when you feel more free to start saying exactly what you think, having somehow developed a 'don't give a fuck' attitude which may in fact be from sheer damn exhaustion, but I think also comes from an unconscious realisation that you may just have been giving way too many fucks about all the wrong stuff. You have to think about what you do in life that gives you gain, and what drains you. Start to realise the Good Girl expectation you were conditioned to be never served you, only others, and being good to yourself serves you (and ultimately, the ones you love) better. Courage means grabbing midlife by the love handles and giving it everything you've got. It's having the guts to create healthy relationships, create a healthy respect for your health and body, and create a nurturing environment around yourself. Go Girl!

Decision #5 – what are my boundaries?

Take a deep breath. You're going to confirm, create and establish some boundaries here. Keep a YES chart for a week. You can do this in a journal, a notebook, or your phone. Make a note of every yes you give throughout the day. Include the ones that aren't even asked of you. As you'll see here, not every yes is a bad thing, so be as honest as you can. Include every single yes, asked or unasked for.

Now mark G for Gain beside the ones you were fully happy to do, or accepting (laundry is a yes, and sometimes it just has to be done), or you felt it is something that gives you a boost as well as the other person. (For me this is bringing my girls a cup of tea every morning. They don't ask me, and often they don't drink it. I do it because I'm making myself one and I'm more than happy to help them start their day well.) Now mark D for drain on the ones that make you feel bad, resentful, irritated, frustrated, put upon, bored. No judgement here, and no blame.

Put a line beside the ones that don't generate any particular feeling.

Now take a good hard look at that list. Is it mostly G? Mostly D? Mostly meh lines?

Now, in a different coloured pen, tick the ones that are/where appreciated or noticed, or you feel made a difference to someone. Put a cross beside the ones that weren't/didn't.

Notice where you are giving away your energy for nothing, or not having clear boundaries of when and why you will do something for someone. Or when you are doing something for a reward you never get. The big one is – am I actually disabling them by doing this and giving this yes away? Can I tough out the discomfort of holding off a yes to enable them to gain better independence/growth? Do I love them (and myself) enough to be disliked for this?

Spend a bit of time thinking about where your boundaries feel comfortable and when they are not. You'll start to realise where your boundary is. List your top five and refer back to them regularly.

SECTION THREE:
Action

MIDLIFE MISSION

Possible

★

Hooray! You've gone on an odyssey of self-discovery, recognising, remembering and reigniting the core of you. You've unearthed the rusty compass of you and dusted it clean. You've pulled up your sleeves, got out the coloured markers, and begun to draw a map of this new midlife landscape, signposts pointing out the direction you want to take, and the views you want to take in.

Now it's time to venture forth, one intentional foot in front of the other, compass and map in hand, a full water bottle (hydration is everything!) and whatever emergency snacks you need for the journey.

Seeing clearly how you want to live your life today, next week and in the future, living with intention and direction, inspired by your desires and dreams as your guiding lights on the path you tread across this new landscape, will mean everything to your midlife. It has to me and to the women I've had the privilege to coach.

We have an opportunity. We have a gift – a midlife like no other generation before us. We owe it to those before us who never had the chances, and the generations to come who will look to our footsteps in the sand, to show up now by focusing on how to live with curiosity, courage and clear intention.

Keep asking: Am I getting enough out of life for the amount of energy I'm putting in? If I had boundless energy, where would I invest it? Is this belief and thought taking me where I want to go? Am I consciously making that choice at the moment? Am I below or above the line? These are important questions as you get into the living with intent part of this book, because your beliefs drive your actions, and your actions determine how you live your life. In the midst of unwanted and wanted, unexpected and necessary changes, you can veer down pathways that bear no relation to the life you intended or envisioned. Keep alert. Be aware. When you realise you are on autopilot, flick the switch and fly the plane.

Without intention you follow the default lines.

Without intention you react rather than respond.

Without intention you blindly blunder through your days, weeks, and then months, until years have gone by with no idea where you are going.

This is your time to realise you can have real agency in your life, to design and implement a life you love, driven by how you want your life to feel, not just look like.

What you do from this moment, matters most.

You can blame life, your partner or the weather. You can point to politics, twitter or global pandemics for not having to try. Ultimately though, unless you take responsibility for how you live every minute of every day, you might as well blame the moon. You may as well go and sit on the moon. I *know* it can feel hard. I have stared at my reflection in the mirror so many times just wishing I could go back to not really having to make the effort. I've slipped on autopilot and cruised at low altitude below the line, just hoping I don't hit anything. But then I remember that that life feels even harder. I look at a picture of my mum, and I look at my girls and I take a deep, deep, nourishing breath, and take back the controls.

There is so much bullshit to deal with in our midlives.

So much responsibility.

So much change.

So much to give.

But there is also so much potential.

So much possibility.

So much power.

So much growth.

So much to receive.

Now it's time to act. With energy, intention and choice. With your boundaries in place, your values in view, and your permission slip signed.

In this final section you're going to start implementing the goals and ideas you've designed. Let's get going.

11

AND *Action!* ★ HABITS

I turned fifty at the beginning of 2020. In fact, my birthday party took place just before the impact of the Covid-19 global pandemic hit home, and our lives would be completely transformed. Which makes me even more grateful for that night where I danced and sang, laughed and hugged, loved and was loved by everyone that was special to me, glittering dress and disco balls dancing in the specially-hired lit up dance floor.

It was always going to be a marker for me. Not just the midlife marker of turning fifty, but also a celebration of where I was, given the turmoil and challenges of my forties. It had been a decade drained of agency and energy, dedicated to the care of others often at the expense of myself, and a desperate search for myself amid the mayhem. Lest we forget gratitude and attitude, it was also a decade where I raised three incredible girls, wrote a book, ran a marathon, cared for my mum, was enriched by family and friendships, graduated college, started a new business, explored my single sexual mojo, travelled, and reconnected with my body with dance, yoga and most importantly, invested in my own mental wellbeing and personal growth. It was a busy decade!

In the year running up to that milestone I decided to use my fiftieth as a finish line, as well as a starting line. The aim at the finish line was to be "Fit&Fab@50" so I would be ready for the next decade of my life in the best physical and emotional state I could be. This did not mean becoming an Olympic athlete with a facelift. It meant being fit and healthy in a way that was achievable given my lifestyle as a busy single parent; being as bold and beautiful as was achievable given my age, lifestyle and, you know, biology; and being as tuned in to myself and invested in my happiness and growth as was achievable given I couldn't go full Eat, Pray, Love and abandon life as I knew it. (I'm keeping that for my sixties!)

What it did mean was taking intentional actions for a full year that would lead me step by step towards a desired, designed state of being, whilst also trying to enjoy those steps too, incorporating them into the step count of my normal life. It wasn't a case of the means justifying the ends, but the means being *part* of the process (which is why that happiness roadmap you did was so important).There was no point in creating short-term habits to achieve some goal that can't then be sustained once I'd hung up the party dress and gone to the bottle bank. My goal wasn't just to be Fit&Fab@50 for one day, but the year, and then the decade. It needed to become a way of life, not a one-day wonder. My midlife redefined, better, bolder and brighter.

This meant looking at my habits and routines around food (nutrition, snacking, alcohol, diet), exercise (strength, fitness, body shape), appearance (hair, skin care, makeup, clothes), energy management (work, boundaries, sleep, bedtime routine, rest, recharging), mental health (gratitude, attitude, meditation, influences, distractions), and behaviours (responses, triggers, beliefs).

The act of actually investigating all that was enough to make me need a cup of tea and a packet of biscuits. But to go from Flabby&Fecked@49 (not really, but not where I wanted to be at) to Fit&Fab@50 meant being clear what I wanted, and then taking intentional, decisive micro actions every day. From researching and committing to a proper skin care ritual for my age, to carving out three hours a week to do a pilates class before sitting down to work; from roping in a pal to run once a week with, to buying flaxseeds and adding them to every smoothie and salad; from deciding to only drink alcohol on Friday and Saturday evenings, to not drinking caffeine after 4pm; from trying to commit to going upstairs at 10pm and reading for half an hour rather than watch another TV show, to making small changes in my housework, every little action in its own right was a slight shift, but put together, and when built up with consistency, it became a significant shift. I was by no means 'perfect'. Thank the Goddesses of Women's Sanity I was in recovery for that, and so occasionally had a glass of wine on a Wednesday night. Remember: it's progress you're after, not perfection. I was sometimes too grumpy to be grateful. I occasionally went to bed early but then drowned in Twitter instead of reading my book. But on the whole, most of the time, for the most part, nine (or eight) times out of ten, all the cliches, I kept the actions going by creating habits that worked in my favour. And importantly not giving up entirely if I had a Wednesday wobble.

And ... Action!

Every action you take is a vote for the kind of person you want to be. But likely your life is ruled by habits; the habitual ways you do things without thinking, yet they define the outcome of your life. The upside of habits is that they allow you to not have to reinvent the wheel every single time you do something – how to set the table, how to fold the laundry, how you start an email, how you exercise.

The downside of habits is the exact same reason. You don't reinvent the wheel and so if you aren't careful (or vigilant), you can perform a large part of your life on autopilot, acting with little or no thought or intention. Some research puts habitual behaviour at 40% of our days. Unless you check to make sure your habits aren't past their sell-by date, you can be behaving in ways that damage or hold you back.

So how do you form these ways of behaving without thought? Sadly, what you usually don't do, is sit down with a blank sheet of paper at the beginning of each stage of your life and decide exactly what beliefs, habits, routines would best serve you to give you the life you wanted to live (which is what you're doing now!). Instead you usually absorb many of your habits – even habits around thinking certain ways about things – from childhood, upbringing, and culture. As children, *you* are the blank sheet, imprinted with programming from parents, peers, teachers, family, friends, and the cultural influences of the time.

As an example, think about something you do automatically like stack the dishwasher. Chances are you do it exactly the way your mum did. I even count the dinner plates out the way my mum did when I'm laying out the dinner. You will form many of your habits without ever thinking about them.

Another way you form habits is by creating them for a specific time, reason or outcome. This could have been when you were a student, became a new parent, or were overcoming heartache. A few years ago I caught myself reaching for the cereal boxes and setting the breakfast bowls out before heading to bed, even though I was exhausted. I suddenly realised I had started that habit when my kids were too young to reach the cereal cupboard. Now they are teens and more than capable of getting their own cereal, but even though the circumstances that had led to the habit-formation had long since become redundant, the habit remained. The final way you form habits is by falling into them without intention because of a change in circumstances like an illness, event, or you know, a global pandemic.

Of course many habits are positive. The point isn't that all habits are bad; the point is that if you don't pay attention, continually challenging how and why you do something, you can do it forever, even when it becomes harmful, redundant or energy-sucking. An example of this is the one I mentioned above: overcoming heartache. In my Year of Living Despairingly, I got into the habit of marking the switch-off point of my day – the point that came after keeping my perfectionist smile fixed all day, engaging with the world before getting my kids off to bed, sweet smiles, hugs and kisses all the way. But as soon as the last light was out, I would literally take my coping face off and collapse, often on the last step of the stairs. To mark this intense feeling of relief I would pour myself a gin & tonic, and attach a nosh-bag to my face to eat a family bag of Doritos while watching some mindless Netflix. And I'm not going to apologise for that. My life was in melt-down and I was just about holding it all together, so I needed that switch-off every evening. For a good few months, and perhaps even the year, that habit was probably what I needed. The problem arose when the habit carried on much longer than circumstances required it. I began to find my feet, began to at least switch on the searchlight to find my mojo, and unfurl from the mental foetal position I'd been in. But I kept having a G&T and eating the Doritos because it had become such a habit, such a familiar way of living, it didn't even occur to me to change it. I think I kept up that habit for a good year or so after I really didn't need it. (I did like it though!)

At midlife, it's really important to check in and challenge your habits to ensure they are still working for you in your current stage, and more importantly asking if they are helping or hindering you to be the person you want to be.

The same for routines. As habits are actions without thoughts, routines are often made up of a series of habits. Routines make your world go round. While they help you establish some sort of order in your life, again, like habits, if you're not aware of them, regularly checking in to make sure they're still working for you, they can actually become obstacles to living a life of design, not default.

Routines that might have worked when you had small children aren't necessarily the best routines now they are teenagers. Routines that worked pre-Covid may not be useful during Covid and then again post-Covid.

Have a think about some of your routines:

★ Morning routine

★ Breakfast routine

★ Leaving for work routine

★ Lunchtime routine

★ Dinner time routine

★ After dinner routine

★ Afternoon energy dip routine

★ Mental health routine

- ★ Evening routine
- ★ Bedtime routine
- ★ Exercise routine
- ★ Self-care routine
- ★ Beauty routine
- ★ Decompress from work routine
- ★ Weekend routine

Some questions you can ask when you're looking at your routines are:

How does this routine make me feel?

How would I like to feel?

What can I change/improve?

Changes don't have to be huge. Small, incremental changes can make a significant difference over time. Success doesn't happen overnight and it doesn't hit you like a lightning bolt. Instead, success – in all areas of your life – is usually the result of consistent daily intentional action. The key is to get off autopilot as much as possible, to check in with habits and routines and make sure that the actions you are taking every day are working for you, not against you.

Often with clients, I help them find a habit they do anyway, but upgrade it by using it to incorporate or prompt another habit they want to form. I call these 'Habit Hacks' and you can do it in a few ways.

Hack an existing habit

My client Julie was trying to build greater awareness into her day. Rather than expect her mind to suddenly start checking in with herself at regular intervals, we looked for a habit that could be used as a prompt.

> ***She isn't changing that habit, but using it as a trigger to create a new habit alongside it.***

This could be every time she goes to the loo, opens the fridge door, puts the kettle on, folds the laundry, sets the table, or finishes a work call. She chose the kettle option and initially placed a post-it beside it so that every time she now makes a cuppa, she's prompted to check in with herself for a moment or two while it boils. The more she does it, the more natural (and habitual) it will become. Julie also wanted to start a gratitude practice, but didn't want to keep a journal beside her bed in case someone read it. So again, we found a suitable habit to use as a prompt. Now, every morning and evening while she cleans her teeth, she uses the time to think about the things she is grateful for. When I decided I wanted Michelle Obama arms as part of my Fit&Fab@50 plan, I balked at the 364 gym visits a week I assumed this would require. As I perused my repertoire of habits, I too chose the kettle. I now keep a pair of hand weights beside it and do my arm crunches every time it boils. (My arms may never look like Michelle Obama's but they're definitely a lot firmer than they used to be. I drink a lot of tea!)

Hack an existing routine

Hacking a routine either removes or replaces an action within it, or adds a new action. It's a bit like inserting new code into a program, or upgrading your phone.

Recently, I decided to create small pockets of quiet throughout my day: little bubbles that weren't filled with noise, chatter, or thinking. I knew that trying to find specific spaces for that in a packed and busy diary was going to make the feat a failure before it started. So I looked at my routines and found a couple where I could insert this new action easily. For example, my morning routine involves walking my daughter to school and then walking the dog round the park while listening to the news on EarPods. I've hacked this routine by delaying putting my EarPods in at the start so I can walk for ten or fifteen minutes in silence with no distraction, listening to the birds to quieten my mind (or I wait until the sports news comes on and take them out). Also, instead of putting the radio on first thing in the morning, I wait ten minutes. Instead of immediately opening my book when I sit in the garden, I wait ten minutes to sit quietly listening and watching the nature around me. It has been utterly transformative, yet it hasn't required a gigantic effort. Small actions can reap big rewards.

Have a pre-habit habit or prompt

Prompts have proved to be really valuable to creating new habits, or staying focused on goals. Because the new habit is new, it's not going to feel automatic. Yet. I might go to bed with the intention of going for a run in the morning before breakfast, but because it's not an embedded habit yet, I could well wake up, go about my normal habitual morning routine before I remember my goal. So until it becomes a newly embedded habit, you need prompts. A pre-habit habit or prompt, like leaving out your running clothes the night before, is one little habit that will increase your chances of succeeding in your goal to run the next morning.

I've a goal of taking a trip to Bali. However, until I started to put some thoughts around it, it stayed an aspiration. I knew I couldn't go for another two years because of money, pre-existing plans and time. I knew in two years my children would be going on a three-week trip with their father, and that was my window. But I keep the dream alive, present, actionable. I changed my laptop passwords to reference the goal. I wrote it down on plans, talked about it, set up a special account with a direct debit that takes a small amount of money every month. Before long, it became a part of my life, just as reliable and predictable as my youngest leaving primary school and going to secondary school. I prompt myself constantly to make it real.

You probably do this with immediate things you want to remember, like leaving an important file by the front door the night before so you don't forget it, or the birthday present you want to drop off the next day. Visual cues are a natural part of our lives, and research has shown that when it comes to changing habits, they work.

Have a habit plan

If you are trying to change or stop a particular habit, it's really useful to have an alternative action at the ready in case Plan A isn't possible. If I want to eat a biscuit, for example, I might create an alternative habit like grabbing an apple or some nuts. Having an if/then plan for habits you are trying to break creates an immediate replacement habit because simply saying 'Stop eating biscuits' might not be enough. (For most of us anyway!) Replacing a habit with a substitute is far more likely to be successful.

So, *IF I want a biscuit, THEN I'm going to have an apple* (then don't buy the biscuits and do buy the apples); or 'IF I want a G&T midweek, THEN I'll have a sparkling water or non-alcoholic gin with ice and lemon' (and then buy the sparkling water or non-alcoholic gin and lemons). One of my clients, Laura, wanted to stop snacking in the evening. I laughed when she said she would literally take a spoon to the tub of cheese in the fridge. So we talked about what drove that habit. Sometimes it was because she felt restless, she said. Other times it was because she was lonely or feeling fed up. So we hatched a habit plan to create alternatives. When she went towards the fridge, spoon in hand, she'd placed a note on the door. It said, 'What do you *really* want?' When she assessed, she had alternative plans. She would go for a walk around the garden, or call her daughter if the answer was restlessness. If it was feeling lonely, she was to go and hug her husband. Within a week, she stopped the habit (and the cheese went off!) and interestingly she and her husband felt closer. We did the same with the weekly glasses of wine. She experimented with a few soft drink alternatives and stocked up. Saying no to the desired glass of wine when you have no alternative is far harder than saying no when you do. Be intentional.

> ***Simple shifts are much more likely to work than seismic overhauls.***

Talk your walk

This is where your language is key. When an action is *to be* done, it feels much harder than when it is already in motion. The simple act of changing the way you think and speak about your actions can take you from standing at the bottom of the hill, to feeling you are on your way up the hill. You want to change 'I want to get fit' to *I am getting fitter by trying to exercise three times a week, and eating more healthily.* Get into the energy now of the place/space/pace you are manifesting as your ideal, and feel yourself already living it. If you design a week where you have created time for you, or are fitter, or don't feel so overwhelmed, or had a purpose, ask yourself:

How am I acting?

What am I doing differently?

How am I spending my time?

What am I thinking?

How am I feeling?

What has happened to allow this to be happening?

What changes have I made?

What actions am I taking?

Try and avoid language that feels restrictive or demanding, such as I should, I have to, I can't have etc. No one likes to be told what to do, even by yourself. Try and avoid those absolutes like 'always' and 'never' that make no room for allowances or adapting.

Say, 'I'm going to' rather than 'I have to'.

Think 'I am' rather than 'I should'.

As I've explained before, your words make your world. Your language can either be a powerful creative force or a destructive, damning force. You have the opportunity to create what you want more of, beginning with your thoughts and speech. You've seen how important it is to develop a growth mindset over a fixed or passive mindset. In the latter, everything happens to you, but in the former, you are in charge.

It's about being aware of your daily actions – especially the automated ones, the habits you commit to, and the small steps that compound into a life of your design (or not). In other words, successful action is about building momentum, constantly stretching your comfort zone and growing, and acting in ways that make your life the way you want it to feel. And in the next chapter we get really specific on what we want those actions to achieve – with glorious goals!

Action #1 – My Midlife Wish List

You're going to create a simple wish list. Don't limit yourself here yet by trying to figure out the how and when. Just be free. (Pretend you've had a couple of cocktails, or even better, have a couple of cocktails. Take your bra off. Let it all hang out.) I'm not talking about goals yet. This is just getting specific about your midlife mission, without having to win the lottery or retreat to a retreat for a year.

Give yourself some headings and then I want you to write *at least* three wishes for each heading. Headings could be:

Mind: dreams, headspace, peace, positivity, learning, permission, purpose, career

Body: health, ambition, identity, fitness, ageing, activities, passions, hobbies

Soul: relationships, joy, direction, spark, passion, nourishment, career

Other heading options could be: Home, Happiness & Health; or Career, Relationships & 'Me'

Hell, use all the headings. Or the headings you used for the Wheel of Life. The key is to ensure there is variety so that you don't make all your wishes about one area of your life, like career, say. Now simply sit with: What do I wish for each of these things? Get as specific as you can. What does it look and feel like? Then when you think you have it, go for a walk and come back and flesh it out some more.

12 SCORING GOALS IN *Extra Time*

★

GOALS

My Fit&Fab@50 plan in itself wasn't the goal. That was the aspiration and, helpfully, a deadline. Fit&Fab@50 was the umbrella if you like, made up of various goals that formed the spokes. I had a dress size goal. A fitness level goal. A nutrition goal. A skincare goal. A goal for how I wanted to feel. A career goal. Having a goal simply means knowing the result you want. In my case, being fit, healthy, happy in life and actively dating by fifty. Then you figure out the steps to get there because – and I know you know this – there can be a lot of procrastination between the words 'I'm going to …' and 'I am …'

> ***Goals are the destination <u>and</u> the stepping stones to get there.***

They inform which actions to take. Knowing what you want gives you signposts because while it's absolutely helpful to know what you don't want, just focusing on that gives you barricades. Goals create the stepping stones between here and there. When I trained for the marathon, the plan was broken down to daily goals, and I knew every day what was needed to progress me forward, even by a mile, towards the ultimate umbrella destination of crossing the finish line.

A goal is simply a plan of smaller manageable actions that acts as a guide on how to make choices. Because it can't be done on autopilot and requires conscious action, a goal is not the same as an aspiration or dream. Winning the lottery is an aspiration. Waiting for Keanu Reeves to knock on my front door is a dream. Sadly.

A goal is planning a trip to Bali and working out how to save for it. A goal is deciding to enter the Hunger Games of mid-aged internet dating by joining a site and putting effort into writing a half-decent profile and making room for at least one coffee date a week. Step one of goal setting is establishing the destination, but step two is breaking it down and mapping the journey. It empowers you as much as possible to start living with intention instead of autopilot, as much as you can.

> ***What you intend to do with your life will only become your life with action.***
>
> ***Goals give those actions direction and purpose.***

Defining success

You've already started to define what success looks and feels like for you at this current stage, and that is what goal-setting is all about. It's about cultivating who you are becoming in midlife – not a virtual version but your authentic potential. Not just the outer Russian doll, but the core. There is a Buddhist teaching I love. A garden is full of the seeds of both flowers and weeds. With no intent, you end up watering the good seeds *and* the bad seeds. Setting clear goals is about ensuring you only water the flowers, and neglect the weeds – those people, beliefs, versions of you that were formed for you, not by you. Water the good seeds rather than trying to be everything to everyone and nothing to yourself. Your definition of success belongs to you alone, and it might be so tempting to think the only path is someone else's definition.

> ***But remember, you are in the exquisite, unique, privileged, scary, exciting generation of women who are redefining what modern midlife looks like so you can be any damn thing you want.***

There is a part of you that really knows what you want – it might make you tense to let it emerge, but it's in you. It might frighten you. But it's in you. You need to listen. And you're going to have to fight those voices in your head (remember to ask who they belong to) telling you what goals you 'should' have, or asking who are you to have such notions and ambitions. But remember, ambition is not just about going up the ladder, or going BIG, with jazz hands. It might be about going sideways. It might be about changing the whole wall completely, taking a rest on a step, powering up to the top, or shifting the ladder slightly. So it is incredibly important that your goals come from within, rather than be a response to external demands, expectations or others' ideas of success. Your skin is not one size fits all. The only person your skin fits is you, and learning to live well in it is your overriding goal. I can't stress this enough, and I know it's a little hard to grasp as we have been so conditioned to see success and goals as a very specific thing – usually MORE, BIGGER, BUSIER! I'm just reminding you that they can simply be what will make you happy.

Many of my goals are about upscaling – my coaching business, my income, my car. But many of my goals are about downsizing – the pressure, time spent being 'too busy', juggling too many things. I want more time for me to be, to travel, to learn, and do fun stuff. I'm bored of the bullshit of what I'm 'supposed' to be and 'should' be, and am finally learning to just be me. During the process of writing this chapter, I've just started learning how to play tennis at the tender age of fifty-one. I'm on my fourth lesson, my arse hurts like hell, I hit a backhand like I imagine an elephant in mittens might, but I love it so much. Am I ever going to play Wimbledon? Do I need to win trophies? Of course not. I love moving my body in a different way and having a laugh with my pal who is learning with me too. If I get to a point where I can hit a ball in the vague area I want it to go, I might think about joining a tennis club. Not to win trophies or compete, but to have something fun to do that is for me, not work, kids, parents, partners, pets, and whoever and whatever else I feel responsible for. But that goal – joining a tennis club and playing regularly – begins with making time for bi-weekly lessons, and practising in my garden (helpfully my dog collects the balls).

It can feel scary (and liberating!) to take a breath and really think about what you want. Not what you're supposed to want. *Not what's only achievable if you sacrifice yourself, your peace of mind, your passions, your quiet time, your secret dreams, to facilitate a role.* Society sets women up to fail by creating such unfair expectations that we can have it all while doing it all, and in doing so, have no time to live a life for ourselves. Midlife, especially through and post menopause, is the time you get to free yourself from the 'fertility function' and give birth to yourself. Just in a less bloody way. You get to nurture your needs by watering the good seeds and watching them blossom.

The conditioning will constantly pull you to worry about the reactions of others more than the responses you need for a vibrant and valiant life. I know as a partner, there were times that pulled me so far away from my own needs I let them go. As a mother. As a daughter. As a work colleague. And even as a friend. Everything I have learned these last few years, and what I am sharing with you now and through my coaching, is empowering women to push back on that pull. My life is increasingly a response to who I really am and what I need, rather than a reaction to what I think I'm 'supposed' to be and others' expectations. It's not always easy, but actually, as I know from bitter experience, the alternative is much more painful.

Goals have gall

You may measure your days in step count, your watch or phone pinging to congratulate you when you've reached the target you've set yourself. But the mini but mighty steps you take over the boundary of your comfort zone are the ones that really transform you. Your goals do have to be achievable (so that counts out me looking like Jennifer Aniston at fifty), believable and inspiring, but they have to stretch you. You have to want it. Really want it (more than you want the comfort of doing nothing).

In other words, dreams are what you wish for.
Goals are what you are prepared to work for.

You'll likely know of the well-established SMART acronym for setting goals: Specific. Measurable. Achievable. Realistic. Timely.

I disagree to some extent (oooh, having a voice feels good!). At this midlife – this midlife of all the midlives in history – you get to stretch Realistic. You get to define something new. You get to wonder what is possible. Don't sell yourself short. Don't look back in your eighties and regret not creating a life lived for, and about, you. A life that put you at its centre. It feels so risky, doesn't it? But I promise you, that's just history. That's just conditioning. No man ever felt selfish for putting his needs first. Nor should you.

Tomorrow is never promised.
But what a today you have been given.

When you have clear goals, you are making choices and living with intention, rather than drifting on autopilot; you are creating a map of where you want to go, and how you plan to get there. It also means when faced with an old habit or decision (saying no because you are afraid, for example, or in my case, reaching for the Doritos bag) you have a heavier weight on the scale towards something you want in the long-term. Goals help you keep the life you want in perspective.

Make sure they are the right goals

There is nothing worse than an own goal, which is why you need to know where you're trying to score. Often, goals have become a word charged with pressure: the image of flip-chart toting millennials where ***GOALS*** is about achieving and even over-achieving, and it can feel intimidating. No goals can contain the word 'should' in them.

'I should loose weight' is not a goal. It's a bloodied stick that will beat you into stuffing your face even more with Doritos. Instead, 'I want to be fit and healthy so I can feel my best for my fiftieth birthday' is a goal you can get your wobbly behind behind. But even that's not enough. As you will see below, a goal without an actionable pathway is like a destination that doesn't come with a map so you don't know how long the journey will be. In that situation there's always the risk you'll run out of petrol before you get there (and stop at the service station to buy three bars of chocolate and a double cream caramel latte).

Our current culture tends towards more, more, more. But I've learned that often, less is more. Timing is everything and the glory of midlife is that the timing couldn't be better for re-evaluating what's *really* important, or simply what is more important *now*, in terms of what you want to be working towards and spending your energy on.

Life is not a straight line. It's an ever-evolving, helter-skelter, mishmash of pain and gain, growth and setbacks, mistakes and learning, highs and lows, ebbs and flows, and a lot of laundry. It is not a solid pebble; it is the moving sea that rolls that pebble over time. We all grow, and change and evolve, yet often we make rules, reasons and rationales at one stage of our early lives, and then never assess them again. We think we are the buoy instead of the waves.

You will have been wrong. You may need to backtrack. You might decide that a decision you made when your heart was dripping from the murder of young love is actually not going to serve you anymore. You may need to take off the tinted glasses of youth (rose, dark or otherwise) and see things again from where you are now. Goal setting is about making your values and priorities real actions, not just a concept. There is no big breakthrough. Your goal is constantly occurring, constantly evolving, through lots of small incremental decisions and actions. I didn't run a marathon in one day. I ran that marathon one step at a time, over weeks and months, with every ice bath, every pre-run bowl of porridge, every post-run stretch, with every small, incremental action. I didn't just feel Fit&Fab@50 on the day of my birthday. I became it over weeks and months, with every decision made and habit formed and actioned.

Goal scoring

Setting goals is like creating a spell. Only with all the right ingredients does the magic happen, powerful enough to cut through the white noise and mayhem, consciously laying down an intentional path based on your values, strengths and priorities. This is my MAGIC spell:

M – Manifestable

A – Appropriately ambitious

G – Grounded

I – Inspiring

C – Constant congratulations

Manifestable

The goal can't be so broad that you can't put an action plan to it. Rather than wishing for something and then sitting back and hoping it happens, within each goal there are clearly visible actions to be taken, actions that will become habits that become your designed way of living. Wanting to be a writer is a dream. Setting a goal of writing a book by the end of the year involves seeing a plan of action of perhaps writing a chapter a month, which may mean no TV three nights a week, and waking up three mornings earlier. You are creating new habits that will ensure the success of your goal. You've got to be able to see it so well you can almost reach out and touch it.

'I want to be happy,' is an aspiration. The question to answer is 'If I woke up next week, next month, next year and said I was happy, what would it look like?' What would have happened to get you there?

I want to drop a dress size by the summer, rather than I want to lose weight; I want to be able to run 10km by the end of the month, rather than I want to get fit; I want to have upskilled in three areas through online courses by the end of six months, rather than I want to keep learning.

Manifestable – you have to be able to see it, feel it, taste it, breathe it, be it.

Appropriately ambitious

You have to be real. The goals have to be relevant to your life, and ambitiously achievable. They have to push you out of your comfort zone, but not into an alternative universe. Working six months of the year as a holiday rep in Greece is not an appropriate goal if you single parent three school-age children and have a local business. Building a business you can run off your laptop that allows you flexibility and freedom to travel once you have no dependants is an appropriately ambitious goal (mine as it happens). It is unlikely a fifty-year-old woman with an arts degree and no experience will become an astronaut, given the training required. It is entirely possible and appropriately ambitious for a fifty-year-old woman with an arts degree and no experience to go back to college to study business.

Grounded

It has to become embedded in your everyday life, not sitting on a shelf like a book that won't get read. It has to be aspirational yet actionable, day by day. Wanting to drop a dress size in a month doesn't mean anything if habits aren't formed and maintained every day of that month. The actions and habits that underlie the goal are what will define its success. Eating sensibly and exercising regularly becomes a daily habit towards the goal of dropping a dress size. And the good thing about habits? Once they are embedded in your daily life like cleaning your teeth, they tend to become a way of life, not just a separate short-term activity. The weight loss happens as a result of the actions and habits, driven by the goal, and research shows that habits only need about thirty days of consistent conscious effort to become a normal behaviour. Every step you take brings you closer. Even if it's half a step one day, you are further along than you were yesterday.

Inspiring

If the goal feels like torture, your chances of success are about as likely as keeping this woman from her gin bottle on a Friday night. It has to make you want to reach for, but not fall off, a cliff. It has to make you get out of bed, not hide under the duvet. It has to make it worth you pushing out your comfort zone into a new space where you leave behind an old habit, and welcome the newness (and strangeness of change), but not be so challenging you never get out of bed again. The magic doesn't happen in the comfort zone; it happens in the *growth* zone. There may be growing pains but you are taller as a result. I still flinch at the thought of the cold water plunge, but I know that it's only through that plunge that the glory of being a mermaid awaits. If the goal is a 'should' goal, it's going to be a path of pain, ending in a ditch. If the goal is an 'inner gut shouts YES! even while the heart is pounding' goal, then the path may have bumps and potholes, but it's going somewhere worth going. Hopefully with a Welcome Cocktail.

Constant congratulations

They say there is no gain without pain. So make sure the gain is worth the pain. This means that as you build your habits and actions to achieve your goal, the reward of the goal (at some distant point perhaps) may not always be enough to motivate you when the going gets tough along the way. So reward yourself along the way. If I go for a run this morning, not only will I feel great for doing it, but I'm going to make a really good breakfast. If I study for an hour even though I'm tired, I'm going to treat myself with two episodes of Grey's Anatomy. If I don't drink any alcohol during the week, I'll treat myself to that nicer bottle of wine at the weekend. Everyone succeeds with support and congratulations so build it into your goal. Because … you're worth it.

Get Go-aling

So your goal should be something you can see in your mind, touch, taste, and feel so much it's a reality in waiting. It has to be appropriately ambitious for your reality without being limited by it. It has to get grounded in your day-to-day life, not be some added extra you can easily forget to action. It has to inspire you enough to catch your breath with anticipation and excitement at the thought of achieving it, not make you hold your breath in abject horror. It has to be a rewarding experience as well as a rewarding result, with a habit, or series of, self-congratulations along the way.

A couple of suggestions before you start. Writing goals down makes them more likely to happen. Honestly. People have researched this stuff. Journaling, planners, big post-its, notes in your phone, colour-coded spreadsheets, laminated print outs, lipstick on your mirror. However it best works for you, write them down.

They can be personal, professional, creative, healthy, about relationships, exploring, achieving. You have been journaling and reflecting all the way through these chapters, and already have a better idea of what you want to spend your time, energy and focus on.

Here are a couple of questions that you can use to decide if the goals you are choosing are right:

What will happen if I don't do this?

What won't happen if I don't do this?

What will happen if I do this?

What won't happen if I do this?

It's been said a lot recently that you can't be what you can't see. I disagree. It's harder to be what you can't see, but some people have always gone ahead and done it. We are the generation of women defining this new era of midlife so we may have to be what others will see. Whether that's the big, high-achieving goals, or the (I think, riskier) quieter, finding balance goals.

When you want to set goals, make sure you are armed and ready with the most stimulating, supportive, fuck-yes, (hell-yes if you are of a less lurid disposition), inspired, ignited state you can get into. Dance to your favourite tune. Light candles and Om. Take your bra off and wave it around your head. Pour a glass of wine and lock the door. Whatever it takes. This is your time.

Action #2 – Goal setting

Your goals won't sit in splendid isolation, with no connection to your values, strengths, joys, passions, or where your life currently is at. You'll want to look back over the work you did in the first self-discovery section:

- ★ Your Wheel of Life. What needed some attention?
- ★ Your body and health audit. What do you want to (and need to) heal and improve?
- ★ Your values. How do they need to be valued more?
- ★ Your achievements. What made you feel amazing, proud, dynamic, alive and how can you do more of that?
- ★ Your strengths. How can you harness them? Empower yourself with them? Turn them on yourself?

Now look back over the work in the design section:

- ★ Your Miracle Question. What was the life you imagined? What is your definition of success?
- ★ Your self-limiting beliefs. How can you liberate yourself from them? What beliefs are more supportive? What can you do if you no longer believe you can't? What will you do when you no longer believe you won't? What might you do when you no longer believe you should?
- ★ Your growth chart. What is taking you out of your comfort zone? How far can you stretch it? What do you need and want to do, be, experience, have, let go of, grab, feel, taste, touch, smell in this lifetime?
- ★ Your happiness roadmap. What experiences, growth and development and contribution do you want in your life?
- ★ Your boundaries. What do you need to firm up so you can limber up for your time?

And finally, in this action section, so far:

- ★ Your wish list. Your joys, purpose, passions, plans, aspirations, inspirations, desires, dreams?

Gather them all up in your arms (OK, might be easier to put them on paper). Spread them out. Literally. Sit on the floor and spread out each of those pages around you. Surround yourself with the energy and thought you have been putting into your messily magnificent midlife and take a deep, dense, divine breath. Smile. Grin. Fuck it, laugh out loud! Touch them. Put your hands on your handiwork. Now begin.

I like a good colour-coded spreadsheet myself but you can do this in your journal or on your phone. I personally like to print this out and put it on my fridge and always encourage my clients to do the same, but do whatever works for you,

Have your individual goals down the page and along the top columns are:

- ★ the current state
- ★ the goal/desired state
- ★ the actions required.

Activity	Current State	Goal/desired state	Actions

Remember the MAGIC goals checklist.

Is each goal:

Manifestable?

Appropriately ambitions?

Grounded?

Inspiring?

Constantly congratulating?

13

WOMAN ON A *Midlife Mission!*

★

MOTIVATION

There is only one time to start.

It is now.

You are always a work in progress, so there is only one moment when you are good to go.

It is now.

The future doesn't start tomorrow. Everything you do today affects your future, so if you want to sway the future, there is only one time to do that.

As you are now, in all your work-in-progress non-perfection.

You might already be hearing the voice in your head say, 'Ah sure, I'll get going next week when the stars are aligned and Mercury is in retrograde and school is back, and all the wine will be gone, and the cleaner has been, and my boss is on holiday, and the dog has been to the vet.' This is normal. It's your brain's way of tricking you into keeping everything as is, thank you. But as you have now learned – you are the boss of you. You are the boss of you! Relish being the bossiest bitch in town.

There are only two things that matter when it comes to motivation: self-talk and action.

Self-Talk

The worst words you say to yourself are 'When I have …' and 'When I am …' Those vicious little words allow you to delay kicking the ball into goal until you have the right shoes, have lost some weight, have more money, the kids are older, or it's stopped raining.

Just because you've made the decision to make changes, doesn't mean it's plain sailing. There is a voice in your head, so critical, so cruel, so quick to judge, and so pervasive and familiar, you don't even notice it. The more connected to yourself, the more self-aware you become, the more above the line you stay, you will see that feelings and thoughts are not the house: they are guests. Some are welcome and some are not. You are the bouncer.

As anyone who plays sports will tell you, there are always two games at play: the actual, outward game (your actions), and the inner, mental game (your thoughts). Your success has everything to do with the inner game. It doesn't matter how skilled you are, how motivated you are; if you can't win the inner game of thought, your actions, skills, talents, assets, will only get you so far.

You will always have thoughts that want to demotivate you. This does not make you weak, or failing. Just as mindfulness teaches us that success isn't about floating off into a mindless state for twenty minutes, and then unfurling, chilled and smug for the rest of the day; success is catching yourself drifting off into thought, and pulling yourself back. Being intentional is a life-long, daily practice. The key to motivation is not to beat yourself up when you hear your negative self-talk, but to congratulate yourself when you catch yourself, understanding the thought isn't your real voice.

As I once read: 'Falling off the wagon isn't the problem. It's the wallowing around in the mud that kills you.' You will fall off the wagon. That's not a fail, so don't wallow. Just get back up, wipe the mud from your face, and keep going.

The motivation myth

The biggest myth about motivation is that you need it to get going. Research has repeatedly shown that in fact, motivation comes after action, not before.

Just because you want to do something, doesn't mean you feel like it.

This was one of the most important lessons I had to learn. Despite loving yoga, despite revelling in the deep, delicious stretch of my limbs, despite desperately desiring that connection to breath, and despite deciding I wanted to practise yoga at least three mornings a week, the reality was that most of the time, in the moments before, I rarely felt like it. Either I felt like staying in bed that extra twenty minutes, couldn't be bothered to change into yoga clothes after work, or frankly thought getting dinner ready was more appropriate. I had to really focus on the feelings I wanted that yoga gave me, and start with the knowledge that if I always waited until I felt like leaping out of bed like a spring lamb, I'd never do it. That split decision to even reach for the mat was often enough. Taking one step forward is enough to kickstart the motivation, but you'll have to bank on it not always being there first. I've even done yoga in a pair of jeans rather than risk going upstairs to change and lying down on my bed instead!

This is because changing or creating new habits feels hard. You're programmed to like things just the way they are, thank you very much, even if that's sitting in discomfort. The first few times you do something new or differently – ring-fence an hour for yourself early evenings, start walking in the mornings, reaching for an apple rather than a chocolate – will feel forced and unnatural. You can get fooled into thinking then 'This isn't for me' or 'I'm no good at this.' Remember growth mindset? Pushing through that discomfort is where the new comfort sits. In a chair with memory foam; the more you do it, the easier it becomes. When it feels hard, it's because it is hard. Push on. Physically moving sets your brain off on a process of rewiring, and the more you do, the more you rewrite your brain's habit programming.

Wanting isn't always enough. But each time you stretch a little longer, lift a heavier weight, run an extra kilometre, don't react to a trigger but respond above the line, or post a new blog, you increase your motivation for next time.

Motivation is also motivated by clarity around the end result, which is why your goals are so important. Knowing, seeing, feeling, already imagining as a reality – after the action, after the difficult conversation, after the run, after the job interview, after the water instead of wine, after the better sleep – makes starting the action easier.

That's because you are an emotional being, as well as a rational one. You have to be emotionally connected to the outcome, your definition of success. Getting up at 5am to exercise because you should?

Not gonna happen.

Creating discomfort in relationships because you want to grow because you might like to grow, but only if it doesn't impact anyone else, so sorry, sorry, I'll pipe down, I'm fine really, sorry, sorry.

Not going to happen.

You don't have to like every action you take (or no school packed lunch would ever be made). **You have to know what you want enough to take action despite not always feeling like taking action.**

The key is to keep your goals so alive in your daily life, like a beacon shining on the path ahead, so that when the motivation isn't sitting by the front door like a panting puppy waiting for its walk, you know to put your runners there the night before. Putting them on will create the motivation. Opening the laptop will create the motivation to write. Making a shopping list will stimulate the motivation to buy, and eat, healthier foods.

Your brain will always sees change as a threat. You will have to nod to that Wired-to-Keep-You-Safe-Voice that says, 'What's the point?' and then gently say, 'Thank you for your input, I know you mean well.' And then you turn up the volume on your core inner voice that wants her life to feel as amazing as it can be, and say 'Shall we do this?' You have a Team Chat. You listen to fear and guilt and shame. But then you welcome in wisdom, pride and ambition. The more airtime you give the latter, the more confident you will become.

Keep connected to your goals and your brain will slowly start to see change as a choice, not a challenge; as an inspiration, not a threat; as a reality, not a maybe.

> ***The actual act of acting rewires your brain to feel motivated.***

What helps with motivation is its cousin Momentum. The law of physics knows that objects in motion, stay in motion. You use a greater surge of energy starting something than you do continuing something. Yet sometimes it's all a bit of a struggle. You start off with gusto, but then life takes over, and you're back on default mode carrying on as before because that discomfort (and it *is* uncomfortable) is the discomfort you know, and is easier to sit with than the unknown discomfort of trying. You're going to have moments when you want to slip back into old ways. You will slip back into old ways. The key is not to let a slip-up derail all the good work. Perfection is the road to perdition. If you think you've 'failed' because you don't get it right every time, you will stop trying.

Remember, your goal is progress, not perfection. It's not having the odd slip up or moment of weakness that will make you fail; it's the perfection-driven ceasing that will make you fail. Thankfully I'm (mostly) no longer a perfectionist, I'm a self-progressionist. I believe in progress, no matter how imperfect or small.

The sliding scale of goal scoring

I often introduce the Hierarchy of Actions to my clients when they have set themselves some goals. The hierarchy of actions literally lists options and adaptations of the primary goals, that maintains the momentum of the principle of the goal, should the Five Star, All Singing, All Dancing action not be available or doable.

Mary was trying to make several positive changes in her life that had drifted off track. One was to instigate and incorporate more time with her family, and in particular her sister. They had busy lives, and had let their relationship drift. After getting together and realising how much they missed each other, they decided to try and meet for dinner once a week after work. They made the necessary adjustments to home life to allow that – in Mary's case, her husband was happy to take the kids to football and make dinner. In her sister's, she had her mother-in-law stay on an extra two hours. This time became something really special – not only with their own relationship, but for Mary, connecting to a part of herself she had let go of over the last few years. However, four weeks in and her sister had to cancel. Work got in the way. Mary then had to cancel the next week. Life got in the way. She began to tell me it was good while it lasted, but it was too hard to maintain and she almost spoke as though she'd never see her sister again. So I asked her to develop a Hierarchy of Actions relating to the goal of meeting her sister for dinner once a week, but importantly deciding what was the principle behind the goal? Was it meeting her sister specifically for dinner? Or was it connecting to her sister? Obviously it was the latter and so with that in mind, she developed a list of possible actions that could replace the ultimate action if needs be, but maintain the principle. So while meeting for a quick bite after work once a week was the ultimate goal, if for some reason that wasn't possible, rather than not meet, there was a list of go-to options: workday lunch, Saturday morning dog walk, doing their food shops together, a quick coffee and if all else failed, a phone call. It meant that the momentum of the goal's principle was never broken, even if the particular chosen action was.

> ***Don't let the expectation of how your activity should be stop it happening all together if you can't get it exactly right.***

Can't go for a run? Run up the stairs a few times or dance in your kitchen. Don't have time to make that healthy salad? Buy the sandwich but have the salad for dinner. Can't get to the art class because you have to take a child to football? Sit in the car and sketch while they play. The goal isn't the action: it's the intention.

Knowing you can slip a bit makes saying 'I can't' far harder. Do something, *anything*, to keep the principle of the goal going. You don't just decide to have a balanced life (or a bigger life, or a deeper life, or a quieter life) and then put the thought on the shelf to be dusted occasionally (and in my case, far less occasionally than when I was a perfectionist ;-)) The decision has to become a messy, imperfect but living, breathing part of your life today, actioned with habits and intention.

Action #3 – Hierarchy of actions

Look at each of your goals and decide what is the principle behind it. Decide what you think are the main manifestations of each goal (and there may be several). Then simply list some other ways the main aspiration of the goal can be actioned to keep the motivation and momentum going so you end up with a smorgasbord of options.

14

I'M THE BOSSY *Bitch of Me*

★

INTENTION

When I went into recovery for perfectionism (living my life to external expectations of who I should be, and how everything should look), I needed to fill the void in the programming it left behind. I could have chosen many things – slovenlyism, alcoholism, lethargy, voodoo, but I'm grateful every day of my life since that I landed on intention. Intention is a dynamic and empowering decision that comes with knowing yourself, and following what you want and need.

Intention has all of the drive of perfectionism and people pleasing but none of the demanding criticism. Perfection leads to paralysis, whereas intention drives action – imperfect, messy, whatever-works action if needs be. Intention is not goals; they are things we want to accomplish and work towards, but intention is how you want to direct your thoughts and energy in any given moment, day, experience.

> ***The three superpowers of midlife are curiosity (about yourself), gratitude (about who you are and what is around you), and intention (thinking, acting, behaving with direction).***

Like you have now hopefully done, I decided what were the most important things I needed my life to give me at the moment. And then I made it happen with intention, which also reinforces boundaries. Intention connects to a thoughtful why. The more intentional you are, the stronger you will be to defend yourself at the line you've drawn that protects you from overwhelm, people pleasing, abuse, and suckers of your precious time.

Do you want to waste this extra twenty years of life worrying about people and situations you can't change, spending your energy on negative thoughts, hanging out with people who drain you, not feeling inspired, motivated or passionate, accumulating stuff you don't need, trying to be perfect, trying to fit someone else's expectation of who you should be, and what you and your life should look like, on autopilot? I didn't think so. Intention is your new superpower.

Responsible intention

So in that vein, let's go for the jugular. Empowered intention is being responsible for your thoughts, actions and where you focus your energy. The word responsibility comes from the Latin words for 'ability' and 'respond.' Literally, the ability to respond. While you, me and every woman feel responsible for everyone and everything around us, we often feel wholly unable to respond to ourselves because we're already reacting to multiple midlife demands in this hour, thank you very much.

> ***Responsible intention is about being 'able' to 'respond' to your needs – above the line – with positive action and energy.***

Being intentional is not only about making sure you are able, but that you are living with intent by spending your energy and time on things of your choosing. This does not mean abandoning everything you don't love, or no laundry would ever get done. It means building your days, and therefore your midlife, on your terms.

You pro-act, rather than re-act.

You decide the pace rather than race to demands.

You prioritise feelings, actions, energy-allocation, thoughts and time to the things that matter to your midlife: the areas, problems, commitments of your choosing, not of what's chasing you. When so much feels out of your control, focus intentionally on the things you can control. You might not be able to control the external pulls, but you can be in control over how hard they pull you away.

Focus on your body, your breath, your mood. Your health. Your connections to people, purpose, passions and the environment around you. Sometimes when I feel the onslaught of overwhelm – be that the Big Picture Whole Life overwhelm, or a daily-dose-of-all-the-things-I-need-to-do-today-but-haven't-the-required-energy overwhelm – I've learned to pause instead of dive in without armbands, the perfection shark snapping at my heels. I ask am I above or below the line.

I listen to what I need more than what I need to do.

I pause. Break it all down. Decide my intention.

Looking at the one big overwhelming list of responsibility and demands, I can feel like I'm a small speck at the bottom of an imposing mountain. But if I keep my eyesight on the step I'm on and the next step ahead, every one of those steps is manageable. I also get to choose how to step, where to step, and when to rest. I can't be intentional about fifty things. I can be intentional about how I feel, and the thing I'm doing.

> ***Being intentional isn't just about staying in the moment, it's about creating the moment that is going to serve you the best.***

It's about getting behind the day so you can shape it, mould it, manipulate it, steer it in the direction you want it to go, rather than be chased by it like an unfortunate cat spotted by a hungry dog.

Morning glory

The very moment you regain consciousness in the morning, you face a choice. You can stay on autopilot and let the demands and worries of your day, the expectations and the narratives of others, the prescription written by the cultural matrix flood your system, so that you roll out of bed, already a hostage to external circumstances and pressures, your mind already overheating from the worried whirring of thoughts, demands, expectations, responsibilities, to spend the rest of the day reacting to everyone and everything around you.

Or, you can take a moment to set your intention for the day so that you can embrace it on your terms. This doesn't mean those demands and pressures aren't there. It just means *you* are deciding how to respond to them, you actually decide what is of priority to you, and what is meaningless bullshit that drains your energy and has no positive consequence. This is why morning meditations, journaling and gratitude practices work.

You control the emotional narrative.

You decide what it is you need to meet the needs of the day.

You set a tone for how you want the day to go.

That could mean being gentle with yourself, if all around you is chaos. It could mean gearing up with gusto to push through an exciting challenge. It might mean staying grounded if there is a lot going on. It might mean creating or maintaining a certain atmosphere in the house. Whatever the day needs, you are deciding what energy to bring to it.

> ***Whatever is needed, you set the priority. You set your intention for the day.***

It sounds so simple. Yet it's not something we're normally shown how to do. In fact, women are often taught to be the net, seeing and catching all the responsibilities and jobs that need to be done, rather than being the player, hitting the balls. I'm realising this in a different way through learning tennis. As a beginner, what's interesting to me is that the vast majority of my energy and thought is expended on trying to return the ball, reacting to how and where my opponent hits it. Even if I return it, I'm so focused on its power I stay wherever that ball has placed me (which usually leaves me vulnerable to the next out of reach shot). My instructor Matt initially kept telling me to take a beat, step back and give myself time to meet the ball at the place and pace where I can control the return, before running back to the middle to be ready for what comes next. But that felt so risky. I kept hitting the ball as soon as it came at me, regardless of whether my body or mind was ready (sound familiar?). All my focus was on just hitting the ball, not placing the ball. And that is how many of us live our lives.

So Matt gave me an exercise to help me find the space and time to play more intentionally. As the ball came over the net, I had to say out loud 'bounce' and then step BACK! Then to wait another beat until the ball stopped rising and say 'hit.' Then I had to follow through on my swing before saying 'back' to get positioned, grounded and centred in the middle of the court in preparation for whatever comes next. It became a mantra while I played.

Bounce, beat, hit, back.

Bounce, beat, hit, back.

Bounce, beat, hit, back.

The intention of waiting until the ball bounces gives me time to get *behind* the ball rather than try and hit it as it comes at me. That beat before hitting it makes all the difference. I get to choose how to hit it. It feels so counterintuitive at first. I had to train myself to wait because it doesn't come naturally. To let it bounce. Then wait again. Take a beat. Let intent develop. Then hit and let that action have its full moment as I finish the swing, before immediately letting go of the result (not dwelling on 'what if' and did my bum look big in that shot) to get centred for the next return. The rhythm sets my body on a dance: bounce, beat, hit, back. My movements become a focused flow rather than a fractured series of reactions, always waiting for the external to tell me how to behave. No matter where the ball lands, if I keep the rhythm of bounce, beat, hit, back, I have some level of intention and control. Not always. Sometimes a ball comes too fast or too close and I have to bypass intention for instinct. Sometimes a volley is the winning shot (just like in life). But I'm a beginner so

I'm not playing Serena Williams! There is usually time to dance this dance, to feel the pressure to react and experience the transformative results of being 'able' to 'respond' instead. Just as I have learned to do, and am still committing to practising daily, in my real life too. Thankfully Matt eventually let me stop having to say the mantra out loud, because let's face it, that was embarrassing. And in life, it's probably not going to be always possible to hold your finger up when someone speaks to you, gesturing to them to wait, while you say out loud, 'Listen, wait, think what's best, respond in a way that works for me rather than react' before smiling at them and replying. So instead of saying it out loud, and instead of a thousand thoughts coursing through my brain as a ball comes at me, all I hear is bounce, beat, hit, back and somehow the space allows for intention and clarity. In tennis and in life.

Getting more aware by switching off autopilot means you can buy a bit of time to get above the line, so that instead of your brain crashing straight from Trigger to Reaction, you go, with a breath, from Trigger to a rational analysis and reasoning to a Response of your choosing – a response based on the best outcome for you, not a reaction based on the drama of fear, anger and stress.

I have Reactive Alana and I have Responsive Alana. My kids can really tell who they're dealing with. I will often cringe if I've let Reactive Alana let rip, because she is based on below the line, highly-charged emotion, irrational thoughts and unconscious thinking (scared child, hurt friend, defensive everyone), while Responsive Alana is based on above the line, self-awareness, rational reasoning, conscious decision making where, critically the bigger picture and longer-term value is considered, rather then the immediate, short-term reward.

This means the difference between:

Teaching moment with kids (or considering their perspective) versus shouting and nagging.

Empathetic, boundary-led explanation versus defensive, bitchy retort.

A quiet withdrawal to maintain my own peace of mind versus tearing into someone else's drama.

Recognising that you always have a choice in how you respond, regardless of how you feel, will stop you feeling like your mind has been taken over by a room of hysterical, hormonal teenagers who've had their phones taken off them. (If you've never witnessed this, there is no rationality involved at all, just End of the World level histrionics.) Our reactions, pumped up by additional baggage, worry and anxiety are way beyond the rational, self-beneficial considered response to the impact of the initial trigger, because the narrative drama we have played for so long requires it. Get a red pen, and start crossing out some of those lines in your script.

As you are understanding that not every thought in your mind is right, real or reasonable, you can start to take a step back and watch your thoughts and feelings as separate from you. You're seeing yourself as the sky. You're looking down at the clouds – your emotions, coming and going. They are heavy or light, rain-laden or reflecting the sunshine – but you are always the sky. Separate. You can also protect yourself from those clouds, forecast them, bring a brolly in preparation. You do not have to be held hostage by your feelings. Research has shown that your emotions come and go within ninety seconds when you allow them to be as they are without trying to absorb or manipulate them in any way. So take a breath, let them be, and then decide what action will actually serve you.

Your thoughts lead to action. Your actions create your experiences. Your experiences define your character. In each moment you define who you'll become; start this one with intention. Be in charge of your responses.

Setting your intention will change with the circumstances of each day. As I write this chapter, my two teenagers are doing exams. Anyone with teenagers knows that this is like throwing a firework into a box of dynamite. I feel like Dian Fossey in *Gorillas in the Mist*; keeping my back against the wall, making no eye contact or sudden moves, lest a passing comment sparks the flames of the fragile tinderbox of the harried and hormonal teen world. My intention is to keep this household calm whatever it takes. My intention is to focus on the result I want, which is getting them off to school well fed, well loved and not distracted. That means *a lot* of me singing *Let It Go* in my head. The cups left in the bedroom? Let it go. The hostile retorts when you gently ask if they slept? Let it go. No gratitude for making them breakfast and then not eating it? Let it go. This doesn't mean I will always let these things go but right now, today, because I've set the intention that this house (and me) will be a bastion of calm for them, that intent sets the tone for how I think and behave. I'm *able* to *respond* accordingly to how I want, not react to what happens. What I have learned from setting intentions and living as intentionally as I can, what I have seen from the women I have had the privilege of working with who had clearly defined the ball they then kept their eyes on, is that with intention you have the power – you are empowered – in a way you never knew was possible. You can do things you never thought you could do. You can overcome disabling beliefs and create enabling habits.

> ***There are no limitations, no conditioning, no barriers to living the life you set out to live except the limitations, the conditioning and the barriers in your own mind. Intention takes you off default mode where all of these things live.***

Setting daily intentions

While it's important to set your intention for the day first thing, you can also create intentional pillars for your day that will become the way you live. These are elements that hold your day up, so that whatever else is going on, your day serves you the way you need it to. I coach this method because it has transformed my own life. I call it *My MidLife Daily 5* because, like our requisite daily five of fruit and veg for a balanced body, having your daily five of intention will give you a balanced life.

I separate the five daily pillars into:

- ★ physical
- ★ emotional
- ★ mental
- ★ purpose
- ★ passion

You decide what is important to you, what values you want to live by, what – if you had a blank page and could design a day that gave as much to you as it took from you – would be included. I'm not talking about actions here. I'm talking about pillars, principles if you like, of your well-thought out intentions.

What intention are you bringing to your physical self today?

What intention are you bringing to your emotional self today?

What intention are you bringing to your mental self today?

What intention are you bringing to your purpose today?

What intention are you bringing to your passions self today?

So your daily physical intention might be to move, experience touch, be outdoors, exercise, breathe.

Your daily emotional intention might be to connect, practise self-love, nourish, find calm, be happy.

Your daily mental intention might be to find pockets of peace, rest, stimulate, disconnect, reflection.

Your daily purpose intention might be learn, create, build, teach, family, connect, love.

Your daily passion intention might be experience or practise music, art, water, nature, challenge, a hobby.

Remember, these aren't specific actions. They are intentional principles to be applied in whatever way works that day. So my own daily five, formed from my values, my goals, my needs, my desired way to live, are Move, Nourish, Connect, Create and Learn. These five intentions form the basis of every day; I have to live and experience them intentionally every day.

So with Move as my physical element, in any given day this could be a run, yoga, tennis, walk or even a dance in my kitchen. The key is that I intentionally incorporate some form of movement every day, no matter what.

If I made my intention a specific action and then hurt my leg, or it rains and I can't do that specific action, I limit myself. But giving myself the daily intention of moving means I can adapt the action but keep the intention. With that intention, I make a commitment to myself to include movement in some shape or form into each and every day.

Create is my passion element. This could be anything from writing, baking, gardening, decorating. Creating is something that really nourishes my soul, but if I keep it to a hobby, I'll be lucky if I get it done once a month. Setting a daily intention of tapping into my creativity every day means it becomes a way of living, not an added extra. If your passion is music, this could be actioned in a myriad of ways throughout a week – listening, watching, playing, sharing, writing, learning, discovering something new. If a passion element is art, actions could include drawing, attending an art class, reading an art magazine, visiting a gallery, writing an art blog, taking photos, sketching on your walk. The key is you include art as a daily practice in whatever form works for you that day.

I have nourish as my emotional element. This can mean food, a treat, meditation, journaling or time out to chat with a pal. But every day I set the intention to include nourishment for me as an empowered choice. Setting your intentional pillars for the day means that everything that matters to you doesn't come last. They become a priority of your everyday life.

Time and energy management

I need to mention the elephant in the room. Time. For women, this is our most prized possession, yet it is something we feel we desperately lack. We have to break out of the patriarchal conditioning that our sole purpose is to facilitate the lives of others, and that time for us is only allowed after everything else is done.

Whenever I struggle with guilt and worry about taking time for my own personal development, I think of how I want my daughters to live their lives. Historically, like the women before them, do I want them to believe their needs are secondary to everyone else's? Or do I want them to understand they can be loving, nurturing, dynamic, ambitious, kind and generous women but only if they are also fulfilled, engaged and see their own value? Then I put down the hoover and sit and read my book.

Many women believe that they have to be elegantly sipping a Pina Colada, hot feet cooling in lapping water, a shimmering kaftan that doesn't make their bum look big, fluttering in the warm breeze over freshly waxed, recently exfoliated, shimmer moisturised legs, thoughtless-head flung back to enjoy the sun on their freshly chemical-peeled (factor 50'd) face *before* they can invest time and thought in themselves. They don't realise that the time to do that is exactly when they think their bum is too big in everything, they're dehydrated and their skin is flakey, it's raining and there is zero time in their lives to invest time and thought in themselves. 'Have you seen my to-do list?' is what I often hear. Along with:

Next year, once my kids have done their exams.

My husband is having a hard time right now so I can't focus on me.

Work is just too demanding right now.

I need to focus on my parents right now.

It's not the right time.

I'm too busy.

You might think about time as a constraint. But it is the atmosphere you are breathing in, something you own, rather than something that owns you. You don't have much of it. Days fly by like nothing. So you really have to focus on what's most important, avoid nonsense, being really intentional about how you spend your time and manage your energy. This doesn't mean not doing the laundry. It means not doing the laundry with resentment. It means accepting the laundry needs to be done, and then either controlling or influencing who does the laundry, and if it's you, being intentional about using the time, to have positive thoughts, or only doing it at a time when you've done the things that really matter first.

> ***Time is a resource, yet often we allow external powers to dictate it. Being intentional about how you allocate your energy means you dictate it.***

My client Liz had two young children, and was desperate to find some time for herself. When I asked her to keep track of her time, we discovered that every morning after she dropped the kids to their playschool, she would come home, clear up and prepare dinner before heading back to get them again. The afternoons were spent doing stuff with the kids, and then her husband came home and it was time for him. So I asked her why she used the three hours in the morning when the kids were at playschool to do housework. She told me it had to get done and that was the only available time to do it. Yes, but why use what was clearly a golden time for her to do the reading she wanted to do, cleaning? On so many levels this wasn't good for anyone. The kids always saw, and would eventually have an expectation, that the house was always miraculously clean and tidy. She was wasting precious energy on activities that could be done another time. I asked her to make a chart of the golden, silver and bronze time the kids needed her. Golden was when they needed her as her – maybe that morning connection, those bedtime cuddles. Silver was when they needed her, or someone signifiant, but with the caveat that they could also be doing other things. And bronze was basically when they needed someone to stop them playing with knives but it didn't really matter who – watching TV or playing in their rooms.

There was plenty of silver and bronze time during the day, time when she was present but could be doing something else – like housework, say. She could even include them in the housework, making a game of it, and showing them how things get put away, and cleaned up. I have learned never to so much as pick up a cup in my house when my girls aren't with me. Housework can be done while you fulfil the dual role of 'basic parent in the house, little attention required'. I had another client who wanted to spend more time with her partner as they were both busy with work and hobbies. Again, I asked her to make out a golden, silver and bronze chart for her week – golden being quality alone time, or doing something she loved, silver being doing something but with a caveat she could be disturbed, and bronze time being when she couldn't really focus on herself. I asked her to do one for him, and then see where the overlaps were. How could they allocate their energy and time better to make their charts more compatible?

I used to think I 'should' write in the evenings when my work and housework was done. But when my kids were younger, that was exactly when they wanted me to read to them, and give them quality time at bedtime. I would end up so frustrated because I was trying to find my golden time at the exact same time as their golden time with me. Also, when I did an energy check, I realised I am most energetic and creative in the first part of the day, and not particularly sharp past about 5pm. I was trying to do something for me, at the worst possible time in terms of time and energy. So I changed my allocation of energy and time. I did chores and non-thinking stuff in the evening, became intentional with the girls at bedtime, and then got up early and wrote in the mornings. We all have energy flows throughout the day. Without becoming aware of when you are feeling your most and least energetic, and being intentional about then how you choose to spend that time, you can make life really difficult for yourself.

We sometimes think having a 'balanced life' is about some sort of percentage equation between work and lifestyle. But balance is really about understanding and managing your energy flow. Everyone's is different and it changes according to age, season, sleep and activity levels. Understanding when you are most energetic, when you have dips, what boosts you and what drains you, helps you be far more intentional about how you plan your time. Balance therefore is about having a state of mind that is clear, focused, and in tune with how much you have to do and how you do it.

Balance is when your input matches your output.

When our lives are unbalanced, that's when we feel stressed, overwhelmed, resentful, anxious, drained, and have no control. When we have balance, we can still have a lot on our plate, but we feel relaxed, in flow, the juggle isn't so much of a struggle. There is space in our heads to make considered decisions, rather than a blind fog of frantic thoughts and worries, with too many questions and not enough answers.

Really get curious about how you feel throughout the day. When do you dip, why do you dip, when is your brain clear, when does it start to clog up, when do you feel resilient and when do you feel like you want to hide under a duvet. Really notice how your energy flows and what can drain it in an instant, and what can lift it. Balance is getting courageous around holding your boundaries firm, fixing the energy leaks, protecting the energy producers. Balance is being as intentional as you can around directing your energy to the things that matter most. And then making it a daily practice. Balance, energy flow, time management – they're not a once-fixed solution. With intention, they are addressed and adapted daily.

Intentional attention

Time and again I talk to women who want to roar but are afraid to make a noise. Often it is sheer frustration at not being able to get what they need from the day. Being intentional means you give your day a fighting chance of giving back to you as much as it takes from you. We have been so conditioned to please, nurture, smile, put others' needs first, we need to work extra hard to give ourselves the permission to nurture ourselves. We need to act with intent.

Life is too short, even with all this extra time. So live large, be bold, get on the plane, ask for the order, follow your passion, pursue your dreams, speak up, embarrass yourself and get a great story in return. Live with intent.

For me, single parenting is really hard. Parenting in general is hard. Marriage is hard. Caring for parents is hard. Balancing work and home is hard. Whatever you do, there will be elements that are hard. Regardless of who you have in your life, you have to be the hand on your own back, gently offering support and gently guiding you towards a fulfilling, vibrant life.

I wake up every morning and re-commit to intention, to curiosity, to gratitude. Because I know how much harder life feels in the long run when I don't. Every day, I have to invest in that decision to be as intentional as I can be, just like every day I invest in my teeth by brushing them. You don't brush your teeth once. The day's food and dirt accumulates and so every single day you have to intentionally clear the surfaces to keep them working at their best. Your mind is exactly the same.

> ***Plaque is the same as the plague of thoughts and external pressures that attack your peace of mind. Every day is a decision to keep cleaning away the debris.***

I think about my mum, and all the generations of women before her. They had so little time, awareness or permission to invest in themselves. Can I change that narrative? Can I break that cycle? Yes. Can I show my daughters how I can show love to them, others, *and* myself? Yes. Can I teach them the importance of courage, confidence and curiosity? Yes, but only by living with courage, confidence and curiosity. And with intention. Always, with intention.

One of my favourite memories of my mum is of us often sitting in the garden chatting, our faces turned to the sun. I want to make sure not just to turn my face, but my aspect to the sun. You will always face the hardship. Turn your aspect to the sunshine, with intention. It takes intention because your brain is wired to seek danger. Wired to stay safe. Wired to be cautious. Wired to people please and stay in the tribe. You have to intentionally rewire your brain to step outside the cave of your comfort zone. You have to be intentional about not constantly reacting to the cultural criticisms, but to respond in ways that feel authentic and nourishing to you.

Even with this extra few decades of life expectancy, you're still not going to be here long in the grand scheme of things. What is truly important? I don't just mean in terms of the bucket list items. I mean in terms of love and physical, emotional and mental health. How do you want to be feeling? Make those your intentions. You only have so much time in the day, and only so much energy, and only so much capacity to make decisions. So what will you do with your time? How will you direct your energy?

Action #4 – My Midlife Daily 5

Ask yourself:

- ★ What's important to me?
- ★ What habits will make me feel good today?
- ★ What habits will ensure my goals and dreams are in sight?
- ★ If I could wake up tomorrow and my day was meaningful and nurturing of me, what would be different?

Decide your elements

Try and decide your elements based on how you want your life to feel today, and how you want to grow and develop, and any ambitions and goals you have. These could include (but are not restricted to):

- ★ Move
- ★ Learn
- ★ Spirituality
- ★ Energy
- ★ Peace
- ★ Love
- ★ Play
- ★ Silence
- ★ Disconnnect
- ★ Reflection
- ★ Learn
- ★ Create
- ★ Connect
- ★ Explore
- ★ Push myself
- ★ Laugh
- ★ Art
- ★ Passion
- ★ Rest
- ★ Touch
- ★ Challenge
- ★ Me-Time
- ★ Community
- ★ Family time
- ★ Nourish
- ★ Breathe
- ★ Nature
- ★ Music

The Actions relating to each Element

The actions for each element can be varied throughout a week. It is the guiding principle that matters.

My Physical element is ______________________________

____

Actions:

My Emotional element is ____________________________

____

Actions:

My Mental element is ______________________________

____

Actions:

My Purpose element is ______________________________

____

Actions:

My Passion element is ______________________________

____

Actions:

15

I *Love Myself!*

SELF-COMPASSION

I want to finish with compassion.

Because I want you to start with compassion. Every day of your better, brighter and bolder midlife.

Every line in this book was a line I needed to read when I started to piece myself back together. Not just from the rubble of a failed marriage that broke my heart, and the loss of my beautiful kind mum, whose hand on my face I miss every day. But also in the years before when I was losing myself in the melting pot of marriage, parenting, career-juggling and parent-care.

Regardless of our particular circumstances, we all face that midlife moment of truth. When you realise you have a choice: stay stuck in the overwhelm and mayhem of doing everything and getting nothing, your shoulders drooping from the weight of all the layers you have absorbed so that your core is no longer visible.

Or; step off the precipice of perfectionism and the Good Girl signposted bullshit lie of having it all, to freefall into the jowl-flapping G force of a new landscape hoping to fuck you have a parachute strapped to your back.

> ***I hope through the soul-searching work you have done through these pages you have come to realise, you are the parachute.***

Not only do you have the absolute right to pursue a life that serves you and makes you feel the way you want it to feel – but you are all you need to do it.

You have your back.

You are the arm across your shoulder.

You are your Prince/Princess Charming.

You are your hero.

You are the scratch to the itch.

You are the father, mother, lover, friend, coach you need.

You are the permission slip.

You are your own parachute when you jump into a redefined midlife, based on your idea of what success looks and feels like to you.

Trust me. Trust me as a midlife woman who has jumped. Who has felt the utter fear of free falling into the abyss of trying to figure out who I am to myself, stripped of who I should be to everyone else. And understanding the parachute is unique to me: a glorious silk smorgasbord, patched together from all the parts of me; the funny bits, the courageous bits, the flabby bits, the flawed bits, the broken bits, the bruised bits, the dynamic bits, the unique bits that quiver in nervousness lest they be told they aren't acceptable, the furious bits, the creative and the challenging bits.

The reflections and discoveries and awakenings you have hopefully developed through this book about yourself will now light the way for you to live a redefined midlife, one of your choosing, where you can be who you need to be to you, before who and what you are to anyone and anything else.

But only with compassion for yourself will any of it be worth a damn.

I think before any woman ever thinks about getting married, enters a long relationship, or just launches into life, she needs to marry, commit and launch into herself. Not literally marry (although I believe this is now a thing). I mean make a contract with yourself (in your head, in your heart, in your journal, on Facebook, or with a full-blown party – it doesn't matter as long as you do it). A contract to fight for yourself, to love and support yourself, to stand by your own side and have your own back. A contract to allow yourself to grow, to be faithful to yourself, to have and to hold yourself, in good times and in bad, in sickness and in health, when the sun is shining and when the shit hits the fan, to respect yourself and obey your desires and dreams.

I was so busy trying to be strong, I failed to see how weak I was being.

I was so busy shouting to be heard, I didn't hear my own voice inside me.

I was so fearful of being unloveable, I forgot how to love myself.

Compassion for myself began the night I stood on my dad's doorstep, crying to be taken care of, the pus of perfectionism seeping out of that abscess, the poison of pretending I was fine rampaging through my veins, the fever of forever refusing to offer the hand of friendship to myself burning me alive. I think of her often. And in my mind I am now standing beside her, my arm around her, telling her she is loved and she's going to be OK.

As I waited for my guests to arrive at my fiftieth birthday party, lights bouncing around the expectant dance floor, I took that moment for myself. I imagined all the previous me's coming in to the room and I greeted them all with love. The funny child me. The scared and sassy teenager me. The defiant and energetic me's of my twenties. All the me's of my thirties, some happy, some excited, some lit up, others depressed, unsure, hurt. The forties me, the broken, bruised and battered me's, and the bolshy, bright and bold me's. And I smiled at them all, because they are all me and they all deserve to be seen and heard. And I looked up to watch the future me's come to the party, their faces as yet not fully formed, because they will all be defined by the me standing there this night. Who does my fifty-five-year-old self need me to be today? What would my sixty-year-old self rush in and throw her arms around me in thanks for? And for a moment in my mind, we all danced together on this dance floor, a recognition, a celebration, and a declaration: that I am going to dance through this wondrous redefined midlife, whether that is dancing in the rain, or face upturned to the sun.

Self-compassion is having clarity on you

I often describe coaching as like putting on a pair of glasses and seeing clearly again for the first time in a while. Everything you've done through this book has been about building a pair of bespoke glasses for yourself so you can see clearly through your midlife, not just the path you want to take, but the magic that's there for you. Living your midlife with clarity is the difference between wading through the stagnated murky waters of mayhem, and swimming strong with strokes of intention towards where you want to go. It means being clear on your definition of success. It means working with your strengths, and values, being really clear about who you are amid all the labels and roles you have.

Self-compassion for yourself is about being clear about the choices you have, clear about your thoughts and beliefs and how to challenge the ones that aren't serving you well. It's clarity around your evolution, your growth and investing in yourself, constantly. It's being clear that courage isn't for the brave, it's for the bold who know that fear is part of life, and will dissolve once you grab the boundary of your comfort zone and push it outwards. Or at least, it won't kill you. Self-compassion is about knowing the kind of moment, day, year, life you want to feel and live, and seeing the actions and goals that will give you that life, today. Self-compassion is knowing when to ask for help, or when you need a buoyancy aid, how to get still when you hit currents that threaten to drag you off course. It means being able to float on your back and enjoy the sky.

You won't know what's coming around every corner, but you will have such a clear internal GPS system, you won't get lost. It will guide you to keep grounded in exploiting and exploring the magic within you throughout your midlife and beyond.

You deserve it. This is your time. This is the time to stop making yourself smaller, physically and emotionally, but to step into your space, take your place, find your voice, never apologise for your voice, stop apologising, sorry, so sorry, for being who you are and who you actually want to be. Being so fucking clear who you are in all your glorious imperfections that the lens you view this midlife through is sparkling with anticipation of your badness, your boldness, your stillness, your complexity, your imperfection (hallelujah!), your ambition, your attitude, your authentic potential, your rawness, your feelings, your emotions, with you directing your energy where YOU want it to go, not where it is being sucked. And knowing that when (not if) you get knocked off course, you haven't failed, you're human. You just reconnect with yourself again with compassion and curiosity, and keep going with intent.

Sorry, not fucking sorry

Self-compassion is not apologising for who you really are and what you really want.

Like you I'm sure, my midlife has been a struggle. It's the messy middle where nothing is certain, everything is changing, and hey, let's throw a global pandemic into the mix too. At times it is exhausting, hard, frantic, overwhelming, scary, hormonally haphazard, unexpected. But it is also enlightening, empowering, exciting, inspiring, fun, funny, fabulously interesting. The only thing that is consistent is me. So I try every day to remember to live by my own GPS and, while embracing all the layers of my Russian doll self, to love, cherish, respect and listen to the core, and to never let her be hidden again.

Because I have lived a time when my core was hidden. I have apologised for not being skinny. I have apologised for being tired. I have apologised for having hairy legs, I have apologised for making a dinner my child didn't like. I have apologised for not enjoying something. I have apologised for saying a meal in a restaurant wasn't cooked properly. I have apologised for having an opinion. I have apologised for being 'too' enthusiastic, and 'too' excitable and 'too' emotional, and 'too' loud and 'too' smart and 'too' in your fucking face. I have apologised for being me so many times I'm surprised I'm still here. I'm surprised the universe hasn't decided I was, in fact, a defect, and vaporised me.

I will never, ever apologise for being me again.

Of course, I will say sorry if I upset someone with harsh words, or thoughtless actions. I will, of course, say sorry, if my frustration and anger makes me lash out and say something mean. I will apologise for being judgemental; for seeing someone wearing something they 'shouldn't' because although that is conditioning, I have to stop it. I have to break that conditioning that dictates what someone should look like to be socially acceptable. I have to stop judging others, because that means I am judging myself and holding myself to standards that just don't fucking matter.

But I will never apologise for the size of my belly, the sway of my hips, the cockiness of my confidence, my well-thought out and researched opinion that is said with the internal caveat that I am always open to learning and changing. I will never apologise for wanting an orgasm before you, thank you, for having a greasy hair day, for making sure my needs are met, for my loud laugh. I will never take their flinch at my voice as an indication that I have done something wrong, for my wrinkles and my cleavage. I will never say sorry for ageing and still being standing. I will never apologise for taking my seat at the table. I will not apologise for asking for respect. I will not apologise for holding my boundaries … for holding MY fucking boundaries! Yet I have apologised for my boundaries so many times. I have smiled and laughed at a man who was making ME feel uncomfortable because I didn't want my discomfort to make HIM feel uncomfortable. I will not apologise for waking up every day, and wanting something for me, while I also, lovingly and with enthusiasm, give love and care to others. I don't know what the future holds, but I know, now, that I hold it in my hands, whatever happens to or around me.

No one has to live your life except you, so don't let anyone, or anything, design it, except you. You are a glorious work in progress. Whatever you want is whatever you want. Just make sure it is what YOU want and then understand that no one else's wants are more important. Yes, you have responsibilities. Yes, you have obligations. Yes, you have a desire to nurture and love. But no, it will not be done at your expense. No, your desire to nurture and love others does not mean your need to nurture and love yourself is less than them, or after, or with whatever is left.

Having compassion for yourself is about simply seeing that you matter. That your midlife is not something that happens to and around you while you hoover behind the sofa. That your midlife happens *by*, and *because* of you. You decide, think and act with intention. You absolutely fulfil all your roles, but you do so dressed as you, not in the uniform of that role.

> ***YOU respond to every trigger, every stimulus, every external event as the woman that knows and holds your higher value of what you want your life to look and feel like, rather than react as the conditioned, socialised, autopilot, traumatised, hurt, afraid, slighted, shamed girl who didn't know herself or have the tools to know better.***

And then NOTHING ELSE matters. Not opinions, Facebook likes, wagging fingers, guilt-tripping kids, and put-out partners. Not tutting twitter followers, not Instagram air brushers. Not the critical voices in your head that you now know aren't your voice.

There will always be people who don't share your opinions, curtain twitchers who have a different value system, and kids, partners and parents who have their own interests at heart (this doesn't make them bad!). You are never going to please everyone. NEVER. EVER. So start with pleasing yourself. Start with being really clear about who, what and how you are, and run, bare-breasted, hair flying, shoeless and sun-kissed in liberation across a field of sunflowers. (This is a metaphor, but please, please, if that will make your midlife magnificent, then go do it.) If you love heels, makeup and botox, wear them all with gusto and pride. If you like runners, T-shirts and elasticated waists, wear them with gusto and pride. If you are like me and love all of the above, revel in your complexity. There is more than one box. You can live in it, out of it, or jump between as many boxes as you like. You can be whoever, and whatever, and however the fuck you want.

> ***This is your midlife and it is the most incredible midlife in history.***

> ***You get to define what it means for you.***

Because no generation of women before us have been able to. Not without being hung as witches, trolled as bitches, or stoned to death by a thousand raised eyebrows.

Having compassion for yourself allows you to let go of external expectations, and this has been a game changer for me. Not getting overly attached to an outcome, but readjusting my aspect to the sun, with whatever happens, rather than stay railing against the loss of the outcome I had decided was the right one.

The idea of a 'midlife crisis' has been debunked, but there can be that slump. This is not a bad thing. This is a wake-up moment when you realise a lot of the bullshit you aspired to was not what fundamentally made you happy. Or you've ticked those boxes, and have a different vision now. Or an evolution. Or a revolution. Or a transition. Or an improvement. Midlife is not just a moment to reassess and take stock. It is a constant process of checking in with yourself, staying curious, staying aware and alert, and keeping your light constantly switched on. It's not about being self-indulgent, that mocked cliche which goads 'get over yourself.' It's a genuine transition into deciding to live more authentically, not the prescription and description handed down to you when you were younger when you didn't know how to live in a more fulfilling way.

Self-compassion is realising that other people's behaviour and actions are almost entirely about them, and almost entirely nothing to do with you. So the only thing you have control over – or responsibility of – are your own thoughts and behaviour. If you stand by your boundary – a boundary that is rational, well-thought through and if needs be, has been well communicated – then what someone else does with that boundary is all about them. If they step over your boundary – that is about them. You reinforcing it does not make you bad, mad or difficult – the three words often used to describe women who don't tow the established (patriarchal) line.

Showing compassion to yourself means knowing what you want and when to ask for help. I had been clear for a lot of my life, and then for a lot of years it got fuzzy. When I looked in the mirror at forty-five and didn't recognise who was looking back, smudged and nudged away from myself by dramas, distractions, successes, failures, challenges, my instinct was to smash the mirror, or find another mirror that reflected back what I was supposed to look like. But all I needed to do was start to wipe away the grime, work through the smudges, make peace with the reflection, and start to smile kindly at myself, warts and all. That has been the single most important thing. Smiling back at myself, being kind and loving, curious, forgiving and nurturing, challenging and trusting to myself.

It's taken therapy, coaching, facing pain, overcoming fear, learning to play, honest reflection, letting go, laughing and loving with myself, building up, growing and investing in me, and showing up for myself every day of this messy, glorious, imperfect, midlife.

Midlife mission

It is so much responsibility to be a woman right now. We are holding torches passed down to us, we are lighting new torches to pass on, and we're doing all this while spinning a spectacular array of plates. We want more back for the effort we put in. We can run on a low level rumble of rage instead of lit-up energy. We can spend so much time feeling overwhelmed to cover up how underwhelmed we are by a life that takes more than it gives.

And often the weight of that responsibility (or as I think more accurately – reactability) pushes out the joy. We forget to play. The pressure to be practical often pushes out the playfulness in midlife. Self-compassion is understanding that you can be practical *and* playful. You can be functional *and* have fun. Your capacity – this opportunity – to live a life rich in joy, connection, meaning, passion, purpose, peace, exploration, fun, creativity, love, satisfaction, achievement, desire, ambition, inspiration, awe – should never be incapacitated by drudgery, demands and expectations that do not matter, in the grand scheme of things.

> ***Having clarity will help you see through the shit; compassion will help you rise above it.***

You might think the external you is the one fighting on the front line, the one who is at the coalface, getting dusty and dirty but putting on your lippy anyway. But she's OK. She's got dirt under her manicured nails and grit in her teeth. She's come this far after all. A bit of Factor

50 and a good pair of therapeutic insoles will do her fine. It's your inner self that need protecting. She's the one you need to make time for, listen to, nurture, encourage, empathise with, support and kick up the arse. You send her out to people please, to say 'fine', to resize and shape-shift to fit in, you send her out to swallow her anger until she chokes, to be less loud until she can only whisper, to small talk and smile when she desperately wants to go deep and come alive, you send her out to keep going, keep going, keep going even when she is so utterly exhausted her chest is bruised with the pressure pressing down on it. And you send her out like that without a loving hug, without love, with judgement – too fat, too skinny, too old, too shy, too loud, not good enough, not smart enough, not pretty enough, not funny enough, not stylish enough, not serious enough, not young enough, not vibrant enough, not airbrushed enough, not deserving of time for her – and then wonder why she feels so unsteady. Would you do that to your child? Your best friend? Compassion means you put your arm around your inner self, tell her she can, tell her you love her and will always have her back. You have to be her fiercest cheerleader, her proudest mama bear. She has been through so fucking much. Not only has the world taken its fair shot at her, but you probably have too. It's time to put down your fists and look at where she is shining her light, and follow it.

My Midlife. Redefined.

I know. Because I once looked in that mirror and didn't know how to speak those words. I feel so sorry for that me that thought it was all on me. My heart breaks when I remember how alone and vulnerable she felt but didn't have the self-confidence to reach out and say, 'I want more for me'. I want to put my arms around her and tell her to breathe. To stop. To take stock. To shed the layers and layers of responsibility she thought were hers. None of it was hers, except to take care of herself, and then from a place of power, relish in caring for the people and things she chose to care for. I shudder at the thought I could still be her. That sometimes, if I'm not careful, I could still be her. But when I cleared the glass, what I saw was that I was there, waiting for me. Compassion allows me to show her that there is always another way.

Am I without doubt? No. But I am confident I've got my own back.

Am I without fear? No. But I know I have courage.

Am I a perfect parent? Perfect person? No. And I've stopped trying to be, because I know that's a virtual vision, and not my authentic potential. I'm not about perfection, I'm all about progress.

When I really think about it, the biggest joys in my life have not been the headline achievements, or the acquisitions, or the prizes in themselves; they have been the moments of feeling – whatever that feeling is, but feeling it thoroughly in its intensity. Of connecting to myself in the moment, of pushing myself over the finish line, of wiping my tears and getting up, of stroking my child's hair in a silent expression of love, of feeling my body stretch in a yoga pose that reminds me my body and mind are inseparable, of walking the long, languishing beach, sand and sea, the same DNA as my feet, of turning my face to the sun and feeling the heat of this wonderful universe on my skin, of belly laughing with a friend, of being submerged in the violent, vibrant green waters of the sea, of taking a deep breath of fresh air, of having an aha moment when something on a podcast or in a book clicks and my self shifts slightly, when I look back and see the circumference of my comfort zone has inched outwards, when I lock eyes with my child, friend, lover, other and feel that spark of recognition in each other, of dancing to music alone in my kitchen or with hundreds at a gig and feeling my pulse pulsate through me, alive, breathing, crying, laughing, screaming, dancing, walking, lying awake in the stillness of the night.

My midlife is and will be a myriad of experiences, each and every one valid, if only I can be present enough to live it fully. So is yours.

I'm not young. I'm not old. And I'm not middle-aged by the standards of which it has always been known. My breeding years are done, my breasts need a little more support, my eyesight is failing me, but my courage is not. In many ways I feel I have just sat all the exams and am now ready to actually start living. As I succumb to the indignities of ending my fertility years I don't feel an urge to retreat, curl up and lament my non-functioning uterus. I feel a deep-seated urge to grab my life, defunct uterus and all, and start dancing. I want to turn the energy I gave to egg production into a production of me. I have birthed my children and I will love and nurture them until my dying day, but I am also birthing myself into a new space where I will love and nurture myself until my dying day. Where my sole purpose is not to produce – work, food, children, comfort. But to flourish.

Your midlife

If you were yourself today, who would you be?

If you could breathe the way you wanted today, how would you breathe?

If you could think and believe in the way that makes you shine, what would you think and believe?

If you could live every moment with intention, how would you act?

Growing up, girls on the whole were given different aspirations from their brothers. We could be confident, but not too loud. We could be accomplished, but not too proud. We must at all times be good. Good being respectful, polite, nurturing, pleasing. As the boys left the house on a Saturday night they were told 'have fun!' When we left the house on a Saturday night we were told 'be careful!' These things stick. Like post notes in our brains, they go from being reminders, to habits, to chains. Ambition is not a dirty word, yet often it is seen as an ugly accessory for women. Being ambitious does not mean you have to rule the world, the country, the office, the home, the kitchen (unless you want to), or that you have to start being an arsehole as you stomp over people. It doesn't necessarily mean earning more (but you can), or going to promotion (which you can). It can also, and it does, mean you can be more ambitious for yourself. Ambitious for finding a more balanced lifestyle, ambitious for being stimulated (be that creatively, sexually, intellectually, physically, emotionally, financially, academically, mindfully, emotionally). What makes you laugh? What makes you feel? What gives you energy? What makes you feel relaxed? What makes you feel rested? Being ambitious for more of those things is as important as being ambitious for being the best you can be in your career, hobby, personal life. Be ambitious about the way you want to dress, look, feel, think, connect, sleep, move, be seen, be heard. Listen to your voice and have absolute faith in it. In you.

Whatever your ambitions are, just be ambitious about getting there. Now is the most important time of your life. If you aren't living it with curiosity, gratitude and intent and prepared for discomfort, it will be gone. Every morning, turn on your internal light, smile at yourself in the mirror and go forth, in whatever way you have designed as better, brighter and bolder, to this reinvented, redefined gift of a midlife.

Action #5 – My Midlife Manifesto

Make a promise to yourself. Your compass, your guide, your reminder, your rationale, your boundary bank, your ambition, your design. Write it, journal it, bullet point it, Pinterest Board it, make a video, and schedule it to be emailed to yourself once a month. Whatever you decide. Decide your midlife manifesto, and then start living it, with curiosity, gratitude and attitude and compassionate intention.

Or, write to yourself now as your ninety-year-old self. What do you want her to thank you for? Because one day you will hopefully be her. And at the end of the day, she is the only one you are really accountable to.

This is your one magnificent, messy, miraculous, mind-fucking, mind-blowing midlife. Live it well, my lovely. Live it well.

Request

If you like this book, and feel it has made a difference to you, would you consider leaving a review on www.amazon.com/midliferedefined?

There are resources for most of the exercises in this book on my website www.themidlifecoach.org/midliferedefined/resources. Please use the Code MYMIDLIFE to access the resources and templates. If you have any particular 'Aha!' moments or make any fabulous decisions or discover some revelations through reading this book, I'd love to hear about it. Please do get in touch via my website, and tell me all about it.

Thank you!

ACKNOWLEDGEMENTS

Writing a book can feel like one of the loneliest jobs in the world. Long lost weekends when the word count was more important than the gin count. Frustrated evenings trying to squeeze out a sentence before allowing an episode of *Ozark*. Dragging myself up to a 6am alarm.

But while it might take a village to raise a child, I know it actually takes a library of people to write a book. A library full of different sections, each separate genres but really, all made of the same materials: encouragement and support.

There is my family section. And my family section is full of bestsellers.

My dad. A poet. An author. The most creatively productive person I know. You have shown me that even at eighty-five, a full life is one of growth and learning. My brother Simon, you have always shown me how to live well. Thank you to you and Charlotte, Ellie, Tom and Alex for being a family away from home. And Ruth. From a child I have always looked up to you, and still do.

There is my friends section.This is by the library window and is bathed in glorious sunlight. Amanda. Brid. Carol. Liza. You are the stars that have kept my night sky bright, and my days full of fun. This section is bursting with other great names, too many to mention, but I am grateful to you all.

There is my clients section. Powerful, inspiring women I won't name but you know who you are. Thank you for allowing me into your wild and precious lives.

Then there's the library book section of my writing community, shelves full of colour and variety. Vanessa Fox O'Loughlin, you don't just write words; you create so many more words through your encouragement and support of other writers. Patricia O'Reilly who first told me to write. So many classmates in many wonderful courses, so many published writers who have given me words of encouragement to keep me putting words on a page. And so many others who write, who support writers, who encourage writers, who make words come to the page in so many ways. In particular, for me, for these words on these pages, I especially want to thank Elaine O'Neill and Sallyanne Sweeney.

Then the section of the library that is a must-read; my personal-growth and support network section. Dervil – you drag me through the pain to find the truth. Kathleen – you wrapped me in understanding when I couldn't understand anything. Maria – a friend, an inspiration and a sounding board for my thought-work. The LEO Women in Business Network, especially Pauline Logan and my Accountability Group – for friendship, mentoring, support, laughs and being there during long lonely days of the pandemic.

And finally, this book opens with a dedication to them, and so it's fitting I end it with an acknowledgement of them for all they have and are teaching me; because my words about redefining midlife are bridged between them. To my lovely mum; kind, beautiful, complex, curious and loving. Thank you for all the love. To my flower-girls Daisy, Poppy and Ruby Rose; my bold, beautiful, creative, kind, smart, sassy, infuriating, inspiring, glorious, glorious girls. I am the luckiest bridge in the world.

Printed in Great Britain
by Amazon

54552483R00119